Praise for *The Daily SEL Leader*

"This easy-to-use and well-researched journal will definitely guide leaders to grow their SEL skills. I am eager to begin using *The Daily SEL Leader*. Leaders who use it are going to be inspired to learn more about SEL, which will positively affect their relationships with students, staff, the community, and, most important, themselves. I can't wait to see the impact!"

—Claudia Frandsen, Director of Leadership Support Services
SEL Community of Practice Coordinator, Curriculum & Instruction
Ventura County Office of Education
Camarillo, CA

"As the importance of everyday social emotional learning is being understood by more educational stakeholders, we are finding that adults need the tools to practice social and emotional competencies in order to model them in their classrooms and with students. The authors have developed a wonderful resource for educators to use that provides them with real-world examples and practices that will accelerate the adoption of these crucial skills. I highly recommend this book for educators who want to advance their practices of social and emotional competencies."

—Jennifer Rogers, Founder
Rogers Training Solutions, LLC
Author, *Leading for Change Through Whole-School Social Emotional Learning*

"Bailey and Weiner have gifted educators with a multitool guide in *The Daily SEL Leader*. Readers are supported through a theory of action, inserting SEL inputs within a continuous improvement cycle, providing daily actions for individuals and teams to practice and strengthen their own SEL competencies, and a step-by-step instructional manual on exactly how to integrate social emotional learning competencies into everyday spaces with adults and students. This book is bound to be a repeat read by administrators and teachers alike!"

—Sara M. Burd
Director of Social Emotional Learning and Counseling
Arlington Public Schools- Arlington, MA
Council of Distinguished Educators,
National Commission on Social Emotional and Academic Development

"I have supported school leaders for more than 20 years, and I have struggled to find a meaningful, ongoing, and frankly, efficient, way to both support principals in their own social emotional well-being and to develop their capacity to develop their teams' social emotional well-being. This is an invaluable tool for just that! With short manageable activities, it guides the school leader through a daily practice of reflection and goal setting that builds not only their personal growth but also their professional capacity for developing the social emotional growth of their team."

—Hae-Sin Thomas, Former CEO, Education for Change Charter Schools
Aspen Fellow and Lifelong Oakland Quality Schools Advocate
Oakland, CA

"*The Daily SEL Leader* is a comprehensive and practical resource that will guide educational leaders to understand, practice, and model SEL skills. This book is written for educators, by educators. It is insightful and functional and will foster impactful leadership."

—Michelle L. Trujillo, Author
Start With the Heart: Igniting Hope in Schools
Through Social and Emotional Learning

"Social and emotional learning isn't just for kids. It's for all. And in particular, it's for school leaders, for whom a normal day requires confidently and cheerfully meeting the unexpected. Wise leaders know that we are truly only in charge of our own selves, and that we can achieve tremendous personal growth by fine-tuning our social and emotional skills. Bailey and Weiner's *The Daily SEL Leader* shows the way. As inspiring as it is practical, this is a must-have resource for anyone serious about being a respected, trusted, and cherished educator."

—Julie Lythcott-Haims
New York Times bestselling author,
How to Raise an Adult and Real American

"As a busy school principal, I love the accessibility of *The Daily SEL Leader*. Written in short, easy-to-digest modules, this book gives me a daily burst of inspiration, grounding me in the core SEL skills that I seek to deepen in my leadership. The focus on reflection and action is key, helping me cultivate these skills in my daily practice."

—Lillian Hsu
Principal of Latitude 37.8, an XQ Super School
Former Principal of High Tech High Chula Vista
Oakland, CA

The Daily SEL Leader

For Sharon, Charles, Connor and Reed who have all taught me so much about the true nature of social-emotional learning.

—James Bailey

For my mother, Ronnie Weiner, who taught me what it means to persist.

—Randy Weiner

The Daily SEL Leader

A Guided Journal

James Bailey

Randy Weiner

A SAGE Publishing Company

FOR INFORMATION:

Corwin

A SAGE Company

2455 Teller Road

Thousand Oaks, California 91320

(800) 233-9936

www.corwin.com

SAGE Publications Ltd.

1 Oliver's Yard

55 City Road

London EC1Y 1SP

United Kingdom

SAGE Publications India Pvt. Ltd.

B 1/I 1 Mohan Cooperative Industrial Area

Mathura Road, New Delhi 110 044

India

SAGE Publications Asia-Pacific Pte. Ltd.

18 Cross Street #10-10/11/12

China Square Central

Singapore 048423

Acquisitions Editor: Ariel Curry

Senior Content
  Development Manager: Desiree Bartlett

Associate Content
  Development Manager: Jessica Vidal

Editorial Assistant: Caroline Timmings

Project Editor: Amy Schroller

Copy Editor: Deanna Noga

Typesetter: C&M Digitals (P) Ltd.

Proofreader: Laura Webb

Cover Designer: Scott Van Atta

Marketing Manager: Sharon Pendergast

Printed in Canada

Library of Congress Cataloging-in-Publication Data

Names: Bailey, James A. (School administrator), author. | Weiner, Randy (Educator) author.

Title: The daily SEL leader : a guided journal / James A. Bailey, Randy Weiner.

Description: First edition. | Thousand Oaks, California : Corwin, 2021. | Includes bibliographical references and index.

Identifiers: LCCN 2020045064 | ISBN 9781071830857 (paperback) | ISBN 9781071842904 (epub) | ISBN 9781071842911 (epub) | ISBN 9781071842881 (pdf)

Subjects: LCSH: Affective education. | Educational leadership. | School administrators—Professional relationships.

Classification: LCC LB1072 .B345 2021 | DDC 370.15/34—dc23

LC record available at https://lccn.loc.gov/2020045064

This book is printed on acid-free paper.

MIX
Paper from
responsible sources
FSC® C103567

21 22 23 24 25 10 9 8 7 6 5 4 3 2 1

CONTENTS

||||||||||||||||||||||||||||||||||||||||||||||||||||||||||||||||||||||||||||||||||||||||||||||||||||||||||||||||||||||||||||||

Visit the companion website at
www.DailySEL.com
for downloadable resources.

ACKNOWLEDGMENTS

Writing a book like this one has always been a lifelong goal of mine but has origins and contributions from lots of places and people I want to acknowledge. My gratitude for all the educational leaders I have worked with and supported over the years who showed me the unselfish consideration of others first without attention to themselves was the genesis of this book. My gratitude and admiration for my writing partner, Randy Weiner, whose creativity and thinking gave new form to ideas I had been thinking about for years. My gratitude to the team at Corwin Press who have been beyond gracious and helpful in our ideas and the design for this book. Last, I owe the most gratitude to my family, both near and far, who have encouraged and supported my reading and writing habits over the years. I appreciate you all more than you will ever know.

—*James Bailey*

I am forever grateful to Dr. James Bailey for offering me the completely unexpected opportunity to co-create this book. I've been incredibly privileged to learn from so many brilliant and diverse people throughout my career. These school leaders, teachers, families, and students fight tooth and nail to support children to realize the dream of being able to live life safely and on their own terms. Ariel Curry and the team at Corwin Press believed in our vision and have supported us far beyond our expectations. Larry Cuban is singularly responsible for shaping my views regarding how to engage in education reform, and I am grateful for his friendship and mentorship. Thank you to the colleagues, friends, and family who've provided feedback on this book all along the way. Finally, love to Pamela, Oakley, and Indigo for the motivation and inspiration to practice being a better person each day.

—*Randy Weiner*

Publisher's Acknowledgments

Corwin gratefully acknowledges the contributions of the following reviewers:

Helene Alalouf
Retired Teacher
New York, NY

Elizabeth Crane
Adjunct Instructor, University of the Cumberlands
Lexington, KY

Jill Gildea
Superintendent, Park City School District
Park City, UT

Pamela Koutrakos
Educational Consultant with Gravity Goldberg, LLC
Author, Corwin Literacy
Wyckoff, NJ

Louis Lim
Vice Principal, Richmond Green Secondary School
Toronto, Ontario, Canada

Tanna Nicely
Executive Principal/Knox County Schools
Blaine, TN

LaQuita Outlaw
Bay Shore Middle School
Bay Shore, NY

ABOUT THE AUTHORS

James Bailey's career has encompassed teacher, principal, assistant superintendent, school turnaround leader, consultant, and superintendent roles spanning Texas, Colorado, and Wyoming. As Superintendent in Wyoming, his district was the first member in the state to join the League of Innovative Schools after reform efforts around personalized learning and social-emotional development. In San Antonio, he led the turnaround efforts for the Carpe Diem Schools. His deep-seated commitment to equity and supporting school leaders led to his training as an executive coach and founding the Leading Learners Institute focused on executive coaching of school and district leaders. He is also an advocate for helping leaders and young people become more self-aware of their social and emotional needs and developing the skills to work with others on a more human level. He has a PhD in Educational Leadership and Innovation from the University of Colorado-Denver, is a prolific publisher and presenter, and currently serves as a core faculty member at Walden University in the area of educational leadership.

Randy Weiner has worked in education and education technology and consulting throughout his career. He co-founded and served as the first Chairman of the Board at Urban Montessori Charter School (UMCS) in Oakland, CA—the nation's first public Montessori, Arts Integration and Design Thinking school. UMCS is nationally recognized for its personalized learning model, winning both NGLC Planning and Launch grants for its middle school model. Randy is also a co-founder and the CEO at BrainQuake, a two-time U.S. Department of Education Small Business Innovation Award winner. BrainQuake's math products have been recognized for their exceptional application of the learning sciences by Digital Promise and are backed by peer-reviewed and published efficacy studies that demonstrate BrainQuake's ability to develop children's problem-solving skills. A Teach for America alum and father to two daughters, Randy taught for five years in Oakland and Madagascar, and holds two BAs from Middlebury College and an MA in Education from Stanford.

INTRODUCTION

We designed and wrote this book to support you in flourishing as both a school leader and as a human being. In our estimation, there are far too few resources available to help you achieve this goal. Sitting in the center of a stakeholders' bulls-eye, school leaders must establish and manage relationships both up and down the school system hierarchy, ranging from superintendents to students and families, and with little ongoing developmental support. It is no wonder that meeting such a daunting challenge is both essential to students' success and also enormously tricky to staff with energetic and engaged individuals over the long term.

This book is meant to be a small contribution to fortifying school leaders' souls everywhere. Opportunities to engage in regular self-care and reflection are too few and far between for you. Our approach here is to provide a manageable daily focus on social and emotional learning (SEL), one of the hottest topics in education circles today, and also a non-negotiable aspect of our positive development and functioning as humans. In these pages, we provide you with examples and simple calls to daily action to internalize and model what good SEL learning and practice can look like for yourself and your staff.

As the heart of any school community, your SEL health will impact the health of your community. Too often, new curriculum rushes into classrooms, with little time to discuss and reflect on the attendant changes new content brings. The SEL trend, we fear, is no different. We see the oh-so-predictable wax-wane-never wax-again cycle already impacting how schools think about the value and feasibility of implementing SEL. However, through self-mastery and exploration of SEL content—content that contributes to a good life both inside and outside the school walls—you can help your community develop their SEL skills and develop themselves.

In fact, we urge you as a school leader to think of your community as you do your students. Your community's members need to be met wherever they are concerning SEL and then nurtured and supported in ways and on timelines that reflect the humanity of learning how to identify and process one's own and others' emotions. So while the book focuses on providing daily SEL reflection and practice for you as a leader, it also serves as a guide for how school leaders can lead their community in its SEL journey. To do that effectively, however, you must first establish an intentional and personal SEL skills development practice, and that's exactly what this book seeks to do for you.

Why Is Social-Emotional Learning so Important?

Since 2001, U.S. schools have sought to increase student achievement through teaching to standards and increased assessment. This approach rests on the long-held belief in the factory model of schooling. In the No Child Left Behind era, and since then, most of the investigation on the influence of school leadership focused on the holy grail of instructional leadership. If school leaders understood instruction in more depth and used newly minted evaluation tools to impact instruction, then all would be well.

Researchers in the field of instructional leadership also sought to understand, more specifically, how school leaders could influence the primary elements of curriculum and assessment, and included a strong emphasis on understanding and using data to change teaching and learning.

However, Leithwood, Anderson, Mascall, and Strauss (2010) argue in a much broader manner that school leaders can and do influence teaching and learning through four distinct paths, three of which actually do not expressly focus on instruction. A path in this sense means the connection of an area under the influence of a school leader and teaching and learning.

- The Rational path includes the technical core of curriculum, teaching, and learning.

- The Organizational path provides for structures, policies, standard operating procedures, and culture.

- The Family path comprises how a school includes and works with parents and the community.

- The Emotional path directs individuals' attention, cognition, and perceptions.

Over the past 20 years of the standards-based testing accountability era, most of the emphasis for leadership development has focused on the rational path (Leithwood & Beatty, 2008), which can also be thought of as instructional leadership. This path suggests that if school leaders were to spend most of their time aligning curriculum and providing feedback to teachers on their instruction or evaluating teachers more strictly, learning would improve. In some cases and places, it did. Other organizational strategies focused on using the organizational path through structures like professional learning communities, data teams, and response to intervention systems.

However, the over-reliance on the rational and organizational paths for improving teaching and learning has led to unintended consequences, adding considerable stress to an ecosystem that was already past its breaking point. Since 2014, U.S. teachers' attrition rate before retirement age rose to 8 % annually, mainly due to challenging teaching conditions like a lack of collegiality in the workplace, input, and support—all factors in the rational and organizational pathways (Carver-Thomas & Darling-Hammond, 2017). These conditions all point to school leaders' need to develop their own (and other adults') SEL practice. This rate of attrition costs upward of 8 billion dollars per year due to the costs of attracting, hiring, and onboarding. Similarly, there has been a 35 % reduction in college students entering teacher preparation since 2014 (Carver-Thomas & Darling-Hammond, 2017). During the COVID-19 pandemic, one survey suggested 20 % of teachers would not be coming back to their positions (Page, 2020).

Surveys of teachers who remain in the teaching profession also illustrate that the field suffers from an over-reliance on the rational leadership paths for improving (LPI) achievement. For instance, even in the pre-Covid-19 2019 LPI survey, teachers rated their working conditions on a 1–5 scale, from highly disagree to highly agree. Only 50 % of teachers in this national survey agreed or highly agreed they had full administrative support. Similarly, 58 % of teachers in the Educators Quality of Life Survey (American Federation of Teachers, 2017) rated their mental health as not good.

Another indicator of the health of the teaching force in the era of rational leadership is visible in surveys of engagement, or how willing a teacher is to exert extra energy in their job. In Gallup's latest study, only 30 % of educators responded as "fully engaged on a daily basis" (Clifton & Harter, 2019). Another survey done by K12 Insight found similar engagement, with only 28 % of educators responding that they were highly engaged (Knoblach, 2019). More striking still, of those teachers with 5 or more years of experience, only 25 % answered that they were highly engaged (Knoblach, 2019). Respondents also rated the overall work environment and lack of feedback and recognition as the lowest drivers of engagement in their schools (Knoblach, 2019). Finally, when asked to choose one word that best described their feelings about their jobs, most respondents listed "overwhelmed" (Knoblach, 2019).

Although school leaders may not be exclusively responsible for the work conditions that confront so many teachers, they are, nonetheless, accountable for attempting to remedy the situation. As the four paths of influence suggest, a more complete school leadership model may provide some of the needed solutions. It is well-understood that the development of leaders' social-emotional skills—a component that may be absent from how leaders use the Rational and Organizational paths—has a high impact on teacher engagement and retention (Carver-Thomas & Darling-Hammond, 2017; Clifton & Harter, 2019; Knoblach, 2019; Leithwood & Beatty, 2008). In their research on effective managers and leaders in all fields, including education, Gallup finds that 70 % of the variance in team engagement is determined solely by the manager (Clifton & Harter, 2019).

In the recent era, the emotional leadership path was probably the least utilized and most underdeveloped. It may, however, be the most promising approach to increasing school quality. Given the repeated finding that teachers are the number one influence on students' educational outcomes (Hattie, 2012), school leaders who fail to adopt leadership practices that directly address teachers' emotional states may be fundamentally misdiagnosing the problem. In a review of over 90 empirical studies of teacher emotions and their impact on teaching and learning, Leithwood and Beatty (2008) found a significant relationship between teachers' thoughts, feelings, internal states, and classroom practice, engagement, and student learning.

The Daily SEL Leader Theory of Action

Although much of the previous few years of SEL focus has aimed at improving students' social and emotional skills, we firmly believe that the development of adult social and emotional skills is as, if not more, important than that of students. People often assume adults, especially leaders, have developed many of the skills we want students to have, but this is often not the case.

To date, little help has been available to you, as a school leader, to understand your social-emotional skills as you enter the profession. Nor has much been developed to show how you might continue to develop these skills, as a school leader, through adulthood. Human growth and leadership go hand in hand. We become better leaders when we grow and continue to build the necessary emotional awareness and abilities for ourselves, and the essential social awareness and skills with others. It is the work of a lifetime. Without understanding why each of these skills is essential to leadership and what the development of these skills entails, you are nearly certain to struggle to develop SEL skills in others.

Our intended theory of action for you to grow in your skills as you use this book follows something like this (outlined also in Figure 0.1 on page 6):

- If you use the resources (the book, additional resources, your experience, deliberate practice plan), and

- If you engage in the suggested activities (daily prompts and practice, note taking and reflections, conversations with others), then

- As a school leader, over time you will have
  - Increased your awareness of high-level SEL concepts
  - Increased your understanding of macro- and micro-skills
  - Developed a more detailed self-assessment of your SEL proficiency
  - Developed more awareness of opportunities and threats in your leadership
  - Developed an enhanced practice habit for SEL skills
- And over time you will have started to create these impacts:
  - Stronger relationships with staff to increase engagement and retention
  - Stronger relationships with families and community to increase inclusivity
  - More awareness of inequities
  - Better mental and physical health for you
  - Increased credibility for leading SEL initiatives
  - Increased opportunities to scale SEL implementation across your school

For Whom Is This Book Intended?

We've designed and written this book to support a wide range of school leaders. By leaders, we mean not only the designated formal leaders in a school like the school leader, headmaster, or assistant school leader, but also others who have leadership responsibilities to work with and influence others, such as instructional coaches, department leaders, team leaders, or directors. Over time, the book could also be explored by other teams or as a whole school focused on developing SEL throughout the school.

How to Use This Book

We'd like to say here at the outset that the most important thing to do, and the only way to get value out of this book is to actually use it. Even if you find that you've heard of the topics we cover in the book before, or you've read some similar prompts elsewhere, we cannot stress enough the difference between reading and practicing. More forcefully, even if you find a prompt to sound trite, the associated action we're guiding you to take will absolutely not be. Developing your SEL skills is not something you can simply read about, and, through osmosis, expect to see results. So, should you come across a prompt to reflect or practice that you've engaged with in other contexts, we urge you to engage with it again here. It is impossible to practice these skills too much.

Figure 0.1 Daily SEL Theory of Action

If you use these resources . . .	. . . and engage in these activities . . .	. . . you should develop these skills . . .	. . . and create these impacts:
The Daily SEL Leader Book	Engagement/ reflection on daily prompts	Increased awareness of high-level SEL concepts	Stronger relationships with your staff, leading to increased engagement and retention
Suggested additional readings	Note taking based on engagement with daily prompts	Increased understanding of macro and micro SEL skills	
Your time, to reflect and take notes	Conversation with others re: self-observations driven by the daily prompts	More detailed self-assessment of your SEL proficiency	Stronger relationships with families and community, leading to more inclusive learning cultures
Your previous leadership experience		Increased awareness of opportunities and threats based on more detailed self-assessment	Recognition of inequitable school conditions
Your previous SEL experience		Increased practice on SEL topics most relevant to you.	Increases in your mental and physical health
			Increases in your credibility when leading SEL initiatives
			More opportunities to scale SEL skills implementation at your school
Inputs	**Activities**	**Outcomes**	**Impact**

Source: Gears by rambo182/iStock.com; Clapper Board by Katsiaryna Pleshakova/iStock.com; Graph by rambo182/iStock.com; and Star by Katsiaryna Pleshakova/iStock.com.

As designers, we spent time interviewing school leaders like yourself and prototyping various iterations of the kind and amount of content that you'll find in these pages. When we first conceptualized this book, we both wanted to include considerably more research than we've ultimately included. Over and over again, we find in our various practices that school communities have precious little opportunity to engage in in-depth analyses, never mind discussions, about relevant research on schools. Not surprisingly, such stakeholders more immediately want concrete suggestions or solutions that they can apply tomorrow.

With this feedback in mind, we turned to our shared belief in meeting learners—of any age—where they are and minimized the focus on research. In prototyping further, we also learned that school leaders generally felt like 400 words per day was the maximum that a book like this should present to its readers. This dosage should take the average reader no more than three to five minutes to consume each day. Again, regardless of what we wished might be true for school leaders regarding how much time you have during your day, we aligned our choices with the lives school leaders are living in schools around the world.

There is an important implication of our design work that we want to make plain here at the outset: Transforming your leadership practice via 400 words per day doses is challenging. This work is involved, deeply personal, and entails making and learning from many mistakes. However, we would much rather provide a relevant, accessible, and usable resource to support you in moving this work forward than create a book that might be exhaustive in its research, but disconnected from school leaders' schedules.

As you'll see shortly, we've made many choices in the book that are meant to help you develop a consistent, long-term relationship with the concepts we present. First, however, let's examine how we've structured each module in the book.

The book is divided into five modules and a final chapter based primarily on the CASEL Framework, with each module focusing on a particular, essential SEL competency. These competencies are the same or similar to what schools are increasingly attempting to develop in their students. In each of the five modules that address the CASEL Framework competencies, you'll find the following structure:

- A brief Module Introduction. These run longer than 400 words. We've applied the 400-word dosage to the daily prompts and reflections, which do not require you to have read the module introduction.

- A case study, based on our experience of speaking with and working as school leaders ourselves, presents a familiar school leader persona. The case study grounds your SEL practice in the reality of your work, attempting to help you see the relevance of developing these skills within your leadership practice context.

- A very brief review of the literature to provide you with background for your work in the module.

- A short discussion of why the module is relevant to you as a school leader.

- Weekly structures that focus your practice on a particular skill.

- Daily entries that include an inspirational or challenging quote, a reflection prompt, space to take notes or journal, and suggested connections to other related skills in the book through the use of a skills numbering system. We have also included a place to note your own emotions daily. You can reference the Feelings Wheel on the inside front cover of the book to help you identify your specific emotions. We strongly recommend that you take notes and/or journal as you engage with each day's prompt.

- You will notice a star by each daily quote. If you like the quote and want to use it again, you can color it in so it is easy to find.

- On each daily prompt, you will see a series of dots similar to a bullet journal design. This space is for you to write, draw, create shapes, or do anything else you need to. The space is yours.

- End-of-week reflections that support you in reviewing your week's work and considering how you might extend it in your leadership practice. Each week we also have you think about the effort you put into learning and practicing the skill and the impact it had on others.

- The end of the module guides you through a final set of reflections and marks the amount of effort you gave during the module and the impact you had. There is also another place to note your emotions as you become more self-aware.

- Finally, more resources can be found on the book's website at www.dailysel.com

Figures 0.2 and 0.3 provide a guide to the two basic structures you'll find throughout the book:

- Figure 0.2: Daily Reflection At-a-Glance

- Figure 0.3: Weekly Reflection At-a-Glance

Figure 0.2 Daily Reflection At-a-Glance

Color in
the star to
remember
your favorite
quotes.

Weekly Skill

Daily quote provides
an additional entry
point to reflection

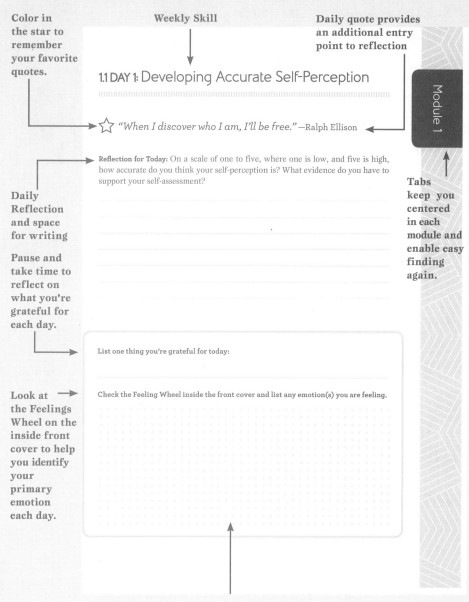

1.1 DAY 1: Developing Accurate Self-Perception

☆ *"When I discover who I am, I'll be free."* —Ralph Ellison

Reflection for Today: On a scale of one to five, where one is low, and five is high,
how accurate do you think your self-perception is? What evidence do you have to
support your self-assessment?

Module 1

Tabs
keep you
centered
in each
module and
enable easy
finding
again.

Daily
Reflection
and space
for writing

Pause and
take time to
reflect on
what you're
grateful for
each day.

List one thing you're grateful for today:

Check the Feeling Wheel inside the front cover and list any emotion(s) you are feeling.

Look at
the Feelings
Wheel on the
inside front
cover to help
you identify
your
primary
emotion
each day.

Use this bullet journal space to write or draw.
Use it for whatever you need!

Figure 0.3 Weekly Reflection At-a-Glance

Day 5 each week will be a weekly reflection of the entire week.

Daily quote provides an additional entry point to reflection.

Color in the star to remember your favorite quotes.

Each week, you'll reflect on a few key questions about this SEL skill.

Use this table to reflect on how much impact you think you had as a result of practicing this week's skill.

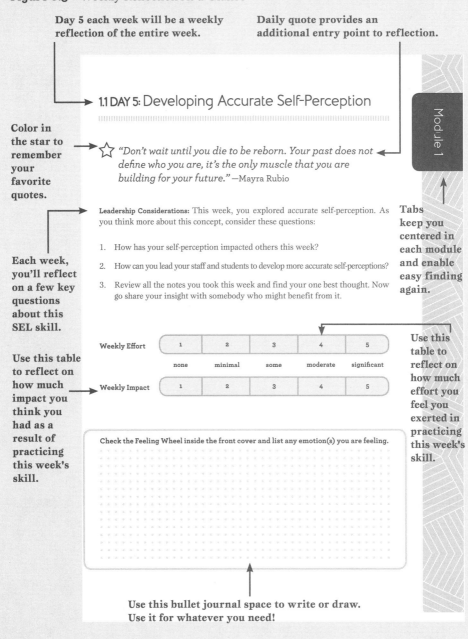

1.1 DAY 5: Developing Accurate Self-Perception

☆ *"Don't wait until you die to be reborn. Your past does not define who you are, it's the only muscle that you are building for your future."* —Mayra Rubio

Leadership Considerations: This week, you explored accurate self-perception. As you think more about this concept, consider these questions:

1. How has your self-perception impacted others this week?

2. How can you lead your staff and students to develop more accurate self-perceptions?

3. Review all the notes you took this week and find your one best thought. Now go share your insight with somebody who might benefit from it.

Weekly Effort	1	2	3	4	5
	none	minimal	some	moderate	significant
Weekly Impact	1	2	3	4	5

Check the Feeling Wheel inside the front cover and list any emotion(s) you are feeling.

Module 1

Tabs keep you centered in each module and enable easy finding again.

Use this table to reflect on how much effort you feel you exerted in practicing this week's skill.

Use this bullet journal space to write or draw. Use it for whatever you need!

With these basic structures in mind, we'd like to share some recommendations regarding how to use the book. We've intentionally designed it to support a range of readers and preferences. We share these recommendations so that you have a place to start immediately, but, of course, you should feel free to customize any of these suggestions and find ways to make the book work for you.

Recommendation #1: Start With the Diagnostic

In Appendix A, you'll find a formal diagnostic assessment that we created. If you're uncertain about where some of your SEL skills might currently stand, taking the diagnostic in full before reading will help you determine specific competencies or skills to focus on first. Alternatively, you might also use the diagnostic as a pre-post measure to see how you have grown through practice.

Recommendation #2: Start at the Beginning

The CASEL Framework moves from skills that are more readily examined and practiced by yourself to skills that demand interaction and input from others. Of course, all your work in developing your SEL skills ultimately occurs within intersecting social contexts. If, however, you choose to start at the beginning with Module 1: Self Awareness, you may find that you'll have an opportunity to build a strong foundation of skills that will strengthen your practice in the even more complex social competencies that come later.

Recommendation #3: Choose a Path

As we mentioned above, each module is split up into weeks, **and each week focuses you on a particular skill**. We have assigned a number to every skill in the book. You can use the numbering system in any number of ways, as you'll see. To get started with the numbering system, you might choose to follow one of the focused paths below. Each path takes you through 40 % to 50 % of the book.

As so many of the book's skills are interrelated, in Figure 0.4 we've identified six different paths, each with a specific theme (there are far more than six paths that we could define, but we think these six, in particular, will provide you with immediate, actionable reading). If any of these paths are of interest, note that you'll move through the book in a nonlinear order, connecting specific aspects of your practice across the CASEL Framework. This particular use of the book is excellent for any of you looking to dive right into improving a critical aspect of your practice.

Figure 0.4 highlights the paths.

Figure 0.4   SEL Skill Paths

Leadership Focus: Increasing Equity	Leadership Focus: Building Trust Through Communication	Leadership Focus: Improving Teamwork
3.3 Appreciating Diversity	1.1 Developing Accurate Self-Perception	4.4 Teamwork
1.1 Developing Accurate Self-Perception	1.3 Developing Self-Confidence	2.2 Goal Setting and Productive Habits
1.2 Strengths of Emotions	2.1 Self-Motivation	3.1 Perspective Taking
2.1 Self-Motivation	2.5 Stress Management	3.2 Empathy
2.4 Impulse Control	3.2 Empathy	3.4 Respect for Others
3.1 Perspective Taking	3.3 Appreciating Diversity	4.1 Communication
4.2 Social Engagement	3.4 Respect for Others	4.3 Relationship Building
4.3 Relationship Building	4.2 Social Engagement	5.1 Identifying Problems
5.6 Ethical Responsibility	5.5 Reflecting	5.3 Solving Problems
5.5 Reflecting	4.1 Communication	

Leadership Focus: Deepening Relationships	Leadership Focus: Taking Personal Care	Leadership Focus: Strengthening Situational Awareness
1.1 Developing Accurate Self-Perception	1.1 Developing Accurate Self-Perception	5.1 Identifying Problems
1.4 Developing Self-Efficacy	2.1 Self-Motivation	3.1 Perspective Taking
2.4 Impulse Control	2.2 Goal-Setting and Productive Habits	5.2 Analyzing Situations
2.5 Stress Management	2.3 Organizational Skills	2.4 Impulse Control
3.2 Empathy	2.5 Stress Management	5.3 Solving Problems
3.4 Respect for Others	5.2 Analyzing Situations	5.5 Reflecting
4.2 Social Engagement	5.3 Solving Problems	
4.3 Relationship Building	5.5 Reflecting	
5.5 Reflecting	2.6 Self-discipline	

Recommendation #4: Create a Path

You might also choose to create your own custom path through the book. Perhaps you'd like to quickly skim through the Modules, note specific skills that are of interest to you, and create a most relevant and appealing path. You could also choose to take the diagnostic and develop a custom path through the book based on your interpretation of your results. Additionally, while reading the book, you might decide that your practice suggests increasingly customized paths, so feel free at any time to stop reading linearly and use the numbering system to support your development of a path that is most helpful to you.

Recommendation #5: Choose a Focus

As you may already know, some of, if not all, the SEL skills demand a lifetime's worth of attention. If you simply choose to focus on a particular week's or month's skills for the entire school year, we would not be surprised. There is much to be said for such focus, especially if you find yourself in need of developing strength and confidence in some of the first competencies and skills that we present. Don't be afraid to give yourself the gift of focus; everyone in your community will benefit from this choice!

Other Elements to Consider

We designed this book to be reused. You'll observe that we did not date any of the competencies and skills, even though we array your practice across a Day 1 to Day 5 construct. Very intentionally, we want you to define when you use this book. You can start using it any day of any school year and repeatedly, year after year. Transformation is unlikely to occur after just one day or week of practice. We want to support your ongoing commitment to your practice by utilizing a structure that doesn't make any assumptions or call for any requirements related to how this work fits into your leadership.

We have also created a practice planning guide in Appendix B to support the development of your SEL habits. There are numerous ways you can link your practice to how you choose to progress through the book. For instance, you might use Appendix B after taking the diagnostic and focus on a competency or skill to build over time. You can add to your plan over time as you connect other skills to the ones you want to develop. We give you brief reminders at the end of every week and module to see if there are any skills or behaviors you want to add to your practice plan.

Or if you want to focus on each competency and set of skills, you could create an action plan for each, which is described in Appendix C. Or if time is an issue, just do the reflections and practice prompts daily.

Overall, we believe that all social-emotional skills integrate and support one another. For instance, it is hard to develop effective relationships if you cannot self-manage what you say to people. As you dig deeper into a specific competency or skill to develop, other skills will emerge as both a cause and effect impacting the skill you want to build. That is normal and the way we grow as leaders. One thing leads to another and back again. To that end, we've attempted to provide you with a book that is part literature review, part narrative, part journal, and part calls to action. The book's hybrid nature speaks to how individual and personal doing this work is; our goal is to support you on *your* path by providing you with a wide range of options to define and stay on that path. We have done our best to create systems and features in this book that you can use to best support your work. No matter how you progress through this book, doing the work, and doing it consistently, is what is essential. We hope that we can make a small contribution to the quality and impact of your leadership journey.

> **Doing the work, and doing it consistently, is what is essential.**

SEL and Equity

As we've mentioned, the main goal this book seeks to achieve is to support you in developing your SEL skills in a way designed to fit into the reality and constraints of your life. We have attempted to provide you with numerous ways in which to chart your path through the book to respect the fact that each reader is a different individual with different needs and interests, working in diverse communities and contexts.

That difference, of course, extends to race.

We want to acknowledge that it is impossible to separate the work to develop SEL skills from the inequities that leaders and communities of color experience. Although we are comfortable stating that all leaders and their communities can benefit from strengthening SEL skills, that work should not always be the same for all leaders.

For example, in Module 4, you'll explore relationship skills. Trust is a critical component in many relationships, and you will find daily prompts that ask you to reflect on how you do or do not build trust. We recognize, however, that leaders or communities of color may not, in all cases, be willing or able to trust white leaders or community members due to centuries of painful, lived experiences when that trust was repeatedly violated.

White leaders may need to work harder to earn trust and recognize that no matter how hard they work to develop these SEL skills, that work may not be sufficient to bridge some gaps fully. It may also be the case that leaders of color working across differences may face a similar challenge of needing to find ways to do the work for students without substantial trust.

We would also like to recognize the demographic reality of our public schools' leadership. In the 2017–2018 school year, 78% of the nation's principals were white, 11% were Black, and 9% were Hispanic. Based upon data from the same year, private school leaders were 86% white, 5% were Black, 5% were Hispanic, and 4% were another race/ethnicity (National Center for Education Statistics, 2020). As a school leader reading this book, the chances are extremely high that you are white. If you are a white school leader, developing the SEL skills we present in the book is also implicitly about increasing equity in your practice and in your community. Using the trust example from above, as a white leader, if you authentically engage in reflecting upon and taking action to create more trusting relationships across difference, you are actively involved in doing the necessary equity work to serve students better.

We want to be explicit that we believe there is a greater need for us as white leaders to do this work than there is for our colleagues of color because the impact of doing so is especially transformative for the students of color we serve. We are confident that all students and all communities will benefit when you choose to engage deeply with the work in this book. However, no matter how flexible, personalized, and accessible we make that experience for you, it cannot be enough. The excessive number of permutations of complex scenarios you encounter every week requires your expert interpretation of what is right and just at that moment. As a leader, we trust you to determine how to use this resource best to advance a more equitable practice given who you are, with whom you work, and where you work when you face those challenges.

MODULE 1: SELF-AWARENESS

How self-aware are you? How do you know? Do you have daily or weekly routines that support your consistent, ongoing efforts to increase your self-awareness? Your success as a leader is tightly coupled to your self-awareness, and in this module, you will have a chance to engage in furthering your self-awareness practice. Quite joyfully, doing this work will help you become a better human being, in general, in those few moments when you're not wearing your school leader hat. In fact, developing your self-awareness as a leader can help you become more comfortable and accepting of your perfectly imperfect humanity, which can increase your trustworthiness and authenticity in your community.

Self-awareness is even more critical if you are leading a diverse school community and especially so if you are a white school leader leading a community of color. Although this book's goal is not to provide an in-depth discussion of the many complex dynamics that are constantly in play when leading across difference, we want to highlight this issue and opportunity. Unless you are already actively engaged in developing your self-awareness, we strongly recommend that you assume that your self-awareness is not 100 % aligned to how your community perceives you. Your goal in this module is to true up that awareness, particularly if you are a part of the dominant culture whose implicit position of power in your school and society may generally affect your self-awareness.

To help you visualize and connect to the concept of self-awareness as a school leader, consider the following short scenario. As you read, think about how the school leader exhibits self-awareness. Following the scenario, we take a very brief look at the self-awareness research base and connect the scenario to the research to help inform your self-awareness practice.

Ms. Jones noticed the time and realized she had only 20 minutes to prepare for a post-observation meeting with one of her teachers. This particular observation had not gone exceptionally well, and as Ms. Jones recalled the lesson, she recognized the familiar anxiety that always arose ahead of sharing challenging feedback. She sensed this anxiety starting in her stomach and moving its way into her throat. Ms. Jones turned her thoughts inward for a moment and focused her breathing on her feelings until she felt calm again.

Following that, Ms. Jones pulled up the checklist of short meeting preparation steps she kept on her smartphone. She liked to follow these steps to ensure she would be present, aware, and sensitive to the teacher during their meeting.

Here's what Ms. Jones kept in her meeting preparation note:

- Try not to speak for more than 30 seconds at a time
- Do not interrupt the other person(s)
- Listen actively; make sure the other participants know that you are listening
- Do not use sarcasm and, if you think humor has a place, double-check the other person's emotions to make sure you are making an appropriate choice
- Speak your truth and your experience and recognize that they are yours, but not necessarily others'
- Seek to be understood, not to be right
- Stay calm and respect others' emotional choices
- Take responsibility; you're the school leader, it's your job

She took a minute and mentally rehearsed how she was going to open the conversation to support the teacher in feeling as much at ease as possible. Ms. Jones typically let struggling teachers off the hook, so she reviewed her observation and feedback notes, made some minor edits and additions, and then ran through them as if she were the teacher hearing them for the first time. This practice allowed Ms. Jones to empathize with the teacher, increasing her self-awareness of how her feedback might land with the teacher. After doing so, she noted that sometimes her tone did not match her intent and that she should pay extra attention to that during the meeting. She also added this to her meeting preparation note for next time.

Last, Ms. Jones took one minute to close her eyes and visualize how she would speak and act during the most challenging parts of the meeting. She saw herself leaning on her self-awareness to present herself as an effective, empathetic, and supportive leader who nonetheless had high standards for her staff.

Feeling ready and as prepared as she could be, Ms. Jones opened the door to her office and invited her teacher in to begin the conversation.

We imagine that situations like this one sound and feel very familiar as they make up the day-to-day reality of many school leaders. Without bringing self-awareness skills to your practice, any situation with a hint of potential conflict can wreak havoc on your emotions, body, and long-term satisfaction. And let's face it, if your work leading a school does not regularly place you in situations with potential conflict, you may not be pursuing enough change for your students.

Research Basis for Self-Awareness

The human ability to be self-aware has a substantial research base, tracing back to the early 1970s. This research rests on the idea that objective self-awareness is the attention we place on ourselves as a social object and that this attention can help us grow and develop.

As with many constructs in social-emotional learning, the meaning of self-awareness has developed over time. Initially, self-awareness was defined as the psychological system that tries to achieve consistency between the individual's sense of self and standards set by that same individual. This system suggested that people judge their behavior, feelings, and thoughts in terms of personal standards or various forms. When a discrepancy emerges between the self and standards, a conflict arises that needs to be solved. However, a more recent upgrading of the theory suggests that self-awareness exists as a metacognitive process defined through its content and form, or the what and how of our internal lives.

Content, or the what, can consist of internal phenomena such as inner thoughts, desires, beliefs, emotions, or moods. Content also relates to external aspects, like behaviors or social relations. Form, on the other hand, consists of how you process your self-awareness through either (1) subjective processing about the self like your self-esteem, (2) defensive processing like feelings of danger or low trust, (3) outer processing of social situations like how to act or adapt in a social situation, or (4) reflective processing based on accepted values and behavior, like asking, "Did I offend anybody with that joke?" (Zabrowski & Slaski, 2003).

The CASEL Framework took much of the research on self-awareness and broke it down into four distinct content areas or internal phenomena. As a school leader, you should continually pay attention to all these:

- Emotions

- Strengths

- Self-confidence
- Self-efficacy

The CASEL Framework also lays out forms of self-awareness or ways for a leader to think about self-awareness, mainly in the subjective processing realm. Subjective processing suggests that self-aware people tend to

- identify some content internally like an emotion,

- recognize the content, and

- make accurate self-perceptions like "I am feeling angry right now."

So what can CASEL's research base tell us about Ms. Jones?

First, from a content perspective, Ms. Jones was highly aware that she was feeling some anxiety and knew from experience that if she didn't minimize it, the teacher would likely sense her tension. Ms. Jones not only labeled her emotion but also identified the physical source, or the embodied notion, of the feeling.

Wisely, Ms. Jones also used a particular tool, her electronic note that reminded her of crucial items that demanded her self-awareness. Simple, quick supports like this increase the likelihood that you will be able to behave in a manner more in line with your expectations for yourself.

Ms. Jones also demonstrated self-awareness in that she recognized where she needed to grow her practice, because she would often let struggling teachers off the hook. In doing so, she made an accurate self-perception. She considered this growth area, prepared what she would say to the teacher, and visualized remaining calm during the discussion. Ms. Jones realized her responsibility, in part, to provide emotional support to the teacher, and so she worked to focus her emotional attention in that way. As a result of her preparation, she created the conditions in which, as a leader, she could have the self-confidence to provide such support.

Second, from a form perspective, Ms. Jones used a personal processing method to identify her more subjective states, acknowledge them, and then make accurate self-perceptions about herself.

Some of the research underlying self-awareness also comes from the circumplex theory of emotion, which supplies a system for classifying emotions (Brackett, 2019). In this model, emotions have two dimensions: energy and pleasantness.

Your feelings can have high energy, such as when you are excited, or low energy, such as when you are depressed. Your emotions can also be pleasant, like when you feel joy, or unpleasant, such as when you feel sadness. This theory is one that the RULER system out of Yale uses to teach students how to recognize and become more self-aware of their emotions (Brackett, 2019). This model of self-awareness can also help you as a leader better process your emotional states similar to the daily emotional check we have added for you as you work through the daily prompts in this book.

Why Self-Awareness Is Critical for School Leaders

Self-awareness research points out that focusing your attention, occasionally, on yourself can lead to more conscious awareness and more accurate self-evaluation. This research supports why reflection and spending some time by yourself is so critical as a leader. Importantly, this is why we designed the book to provide you with short, daily prompts to think and reflect on your practice. The more you engage in these activities, the higher the likelihood you will improve your leadership and your capacity to serve students.

Self-awareness is also critical for you as a school leader because your emotions are contagious. If you are feeling anxiety when talking to a teacher, they too are likely feeling this. If you are not confident when speaking to your whole staff or a team, this energy will be transmitted to them. It is important to note that this dynamic is especially harmful when white leaders avoid engaging in hard conversations across differences in their communities as a result of not being more self-aware.

As you head into practicing your self-awareness skills, here's the main takeaway for why this competency is so essential: You need better self-awareness to be an effective leader. Then, you can start to apply that awareness to interactions with others to gain even more personal insights, including how, as a leader, you impact others. You become more self-aware by focusing your attention on your inner thoughts and feelings, seeking to understand why they are emerging as they are. So as you work through this module, keep these theories and research in mind as you develop your self-awareness.

MODULE 1: SELF-AWARENESS

In this module you will learn more about Self-Awareness through

Week 1.1: Developing Accurate Self-Perception

Week 1.2: Strengths of Emotions

Week 1.3: Developing Self-Confidence

Week 1.4: Developing Self-Efficacy

WEEK 1.1: Developing Accurate Self-Perception

An effective and inspiring leader is aware of their true self to the highest degree possible even if the truth may sometimes be painful. As a leader, when you develop an accurate self-perception, you are also improving your self-awareness. Effective leaders continually interrogate who they think they are based on numerous inputs, including your own and others' feedback and assessments.

A leader who is unaware of how they are perceived, in contrast, is doomed to failure. This shortcoming stems from a lack of developing an accurate self-perception. As a leader, if you do not develop self-awareness, you will never recognize the issues and opportunities that exist, ultimately, to better serve students and lead staff beyond the blinders an inaccurate self-perception imposes.

If you are a leader who believes that developing an accurate self-perception is essential, you will contribute significantly to inspiring and creating a culture of humility, reflection, and persistence. One might argue that when you insist on the development of accurate self-perception and nothing else, you might catalyze more change than any other SEL-related action you might take. Without the opportunity to lead and grow from an honest and accurate self-perception, the likelihood of other necessary changes is diminished.

This week you'll focus explicitly on developing and extending that very skill. We also want to point out that you might wish to move back and forth between this skill and the synergistic skills **2.2 Goal-Setting and Productive Habits, 2.4 Impulse Control, and 2.5 Stress Management.**

1.1 DAY 1: Developing Accurate Self-Perception

⭐ *"When I discover who I am, I'll be free."* —Ralph Ellison

Reflection for Today: On a scale of one to five, where one is low, and five is high, how accurate do you think your self-perception is? What evidence do you have to support your self-assessment?

_____

_____

_____

_____

_____

_____

List one thing you're grateful for today:

_____

Check the Feeling Wheel inside the front cover and list any emotion(s) you are feeling.

1.1 DAY 2: Developing Accurate Self-Perception

☆ *"It's not strength, it's PERCEPTION that makes you stronger. If you change how you SEE it, you'll change how you FEEL about it."* —Yvonne Pierre

Reflection for Today: How have you incorporated accurate self-perception in your leadership practice? If you have not included it, how might you do so?

_____

_____

_____

_____

List one thing you're grateful for today:

_____

Check the Feeling Wheel inside the front cover and list any emotion(s) you are feeling.

1.1 DAY 3: Developing Accurate Self-Perception

☆ *"Self-awareness is the ability to take an honest look at your life without any attachment to it being right or wrong, good or bad."* —Debbie Ford

Reflection for Today: Share your self-perception in a particular area of your practice (listening, speaking, coalition building, change management, etc.) with a trusted colleague and ask for the colleague's assessment of your skill in your chosen area. How accurate was your self-perception in comparison to your colleague's assessment?

_____

_____

_____

_____

List one thing you're grateful for today:

_____

Check the Feeling Wheel inside the front cover and list any emotion(s) you are feeling.

1.1 DAY 4: Developing Accurate Self-Perception

☆ *"The only people who see the whole picture are the ones who step outside the frame."* —Salman Rushdie

Reflection for Today: Identify the aspect of your practice that you feel you have least accurately assessed. Define a plan to increase your self-perception accuracy in this area (suggested simple plans might include conducting a survey, taking a colleague or colleagues out for coffee, hosting a lunch or off-site that invites all participants, including yourself, to engage in this assessment, etc.).

List one thing you're grateful for today:

Check the Feeling Wheel inside the front cover and list any emotion(s) you are feeling.

1.1 DAY 5: Developing Accurate Self-Perception

 "Don't wait until you die to be reborn. Your past does not define who you are, it's the only muscle that you are building for your future." —Mayra Rubio

Leadership Considerations: This week, you explored accurate self-perception. As you think more about this concept, consider these questions:

1. How has your self-perception impacted others this week?

2. How can you lead your staff and students to develop more accurate self-perceptions?

3. Review all the notes you took this week and find your one best thought. Now go share your insight with somebody who might benefit from it.

Weekly Effort	1	2	3	4	5
	none	minimal	some	moderate	significant
Weekly Impact	1	2	3	4	5

Check the Feeling Wheel inside the front cover and list any emotion(s) you are feeling.

Module 1

WEEK 1.2: Strengths of Emotions

|||||||||||||||||||||||||||||||||||||||||||||||||||||||||||||||||||||||||||||||||||||||||||||||||||||||||||||||||||||||||||||||||||

For many years, the development of psychology was based on a deficit model. We lacked this quality or that trait. Psychology as a field of study developed around pathology, dysfunction, and disorders. In essence, it focused on the disease model of the mind. However, in the early 2000s, psychologists began to question this emphasis and started a counter to this called *positive psychology*. Positive psychology calls us to focus on finding our strengths, acknowledging the best things in life, and fulfilling the lives of people with whom we work. Instead of always trying to overcome the worst, positive psychology asks: What does it take to build a good life and flourish? One part of this perspective is to become more self-aware of your strengths—both your emotional strengths and character strengths—so that you can apply these strengths to working with your fellow educators and students.

This week, you'll focus on being aware of your personal strengths and helping others see theirs. The character strengths come from a project done in 2004 called the Classification of Character Strengths, whose aim was to study positive dispositions from history, religions, psychology, psychiatry, and philosophy and pull out those most common across cultures. Researchers (Seligman & Peterson, 2004) found one area of strength is the strength of emotions that you will explore this week as part of being self-aware.

We also want to point out that you might wish to move back and forth between this skill and the synergistic skills **2.1 Self-Motivation, 2.2 Goal-Setting, and Productive Habits, and 2.4 Impulse Control.**

1.2 DAY 1: Strengths of Emotions

☆ *"It is worth remembering that the time of greatest gain in terms of wisdom and inner strength is often that of greatest difficulty."* —Dalai Lama

Reflection for Today: In your work as a school leader, where do you spend most of your emotional time: in the positive emotion or negative emotion area?

List one thing you're grateful for today:

Check the Feeling Wheel inside the front cover and list any emotion(s) you are feeling.

1.2 DAY 2: Strengths of Emotions

☆ *"Strength does not come from physical capacity. It comes from an indomitable will."* —Gandhi

Reflection for Today: From your response yesterday, why do you think you spend most of your emotional time in the positive or negative area? What is that information trying to tell you?

_____

_____

_____

_____

_____

List one thing you're grateful for today:

_____

Check the Feeling Wheel inside the front cover and list any emotion(s) you are feeling.

1.2 DAY 3: Strengths of Emotions

☆ *"Live in terms of your strong points. Magnify them. Let your weaknesses shrivel up and die from lack of nourishment."*
—William Young Elliott

Practice for Today: In your interactions with teachers and students, find three things you find joyful. If you find yourself slipping into a negative emotion, remind yourself of the joyful moments.

_____

_____

_____

_____

_____

List one thing you're grateful for today:

_____

Check the Feeling Wheel inside the front cover and list any emotion(s) you are feeling.

1.2 DAY 4: Strengths of Emotions

☆ *"I was always looking outside myself for strength and confidence, but it comes from within. It is there all the time."*
—Anna Freud

Practice for Today: In your interactions today, continue to find things that satisfy you or give you joy. Mention these to others, and see what happens.

_____

_____

_____

_____

_____

_____

List one thing you're grateful for today:

_____

Check the Feeling Wheel inside the front cover and list any emotion(s) you are feeling.

1.2 DAY 5: Strengths of Emotions

 "We acquire the strength we have overcome."
—Ralph Waldo Emerson

Leadership Considerations: This week, you explored strengths in emotions. As you think more about this concept, consider these questions:

1. How have my emotions impacted others this week?

2. How can I lead my staff and students to consider their emotional strengths?

3. Review all the notes you took this week and find your one best thought. Now go share your insight with somebody who might benefit from it.

Weekly Effort	1	2	3	4	5
	none	minimal	some	moderate	significant

Weekly Impact	1	2	3	4	5

Check the Feeling Wheel inside the front cover and list any emotion(s) you are feeling.

WEEK 1.3: Developing Self-Confidence

Self-confidence may be defined as "an individual's trust in his or her own abilities, capacities, and judgments, or belief that he or she can successfully face day to day challenges and demands" (Psychology Dictionary Online, as cited in Ackerman, 2020). As a school leader, you often use your leadership qualities in various forms to make judgments about situations, students, and teachers. Self-confidence is backward-facing, meaning you gain more and more confidence as you gain successful experience over time. Leaders with high self-confidence trust themselves, have a favorable view of their skill levels, and know how to delegate those areas that are outside their comfort zone. Leaders with a high sense of self-confidence also know how to withstand criticisms that may come their way. In contrast, leaders with low self-confidence often feel afraid of making a mistake or wrong decision.

Developing self-confidence does not mean that you are perfect at everything (an unachievable and unnecessary state, in any case). Under the larger umbrella of self-awareness, though, you know your strengths and what you need to improve in yourself as a leader. Developing self-confidence as a leader helps lessen your fear and anxiety, builds your resilience, and gives you greater motivation to continue trying new things and grow as a leader.

This week as you explore your self-confidence, think about how you want to lead. How can self-confidence enhance how you meet that vision? We also want to point out that you might wish to move back and forth between this skill and the synergistic skills **2.1 Self-Motivation and 2.2 Goal-Setting and Productive Habits.**

1.3 DAY 1: Developing Self-Confidence

☆ *"Because one believes in oneself, one doesn't try to convince others."* —Lao Tzu

Reflection for Today: As a school leader, do you genuinely believe in your skills and abilities, or are you trying to convince others of your capacity? How do you know the difference?

_____

_____

_____

_____

_____

_____

List one thing you're grateful for today:

_____

Check the Feeling Wheel inside the front cover and list any emotion(s) you are feeling.

1.3 DAY 2: Developing Self-Confidence

☆ *"Whether you come from a council estate or a country estate, your success will be determined by your own confidence and fortitude."* —Michelle Obama

Reflection for Today: As a school leader, in which situations or things do you need to develop more confidence? Where could you serve students better if you had more confidence?

_____

_____

_____

_____

_____

List one thing you're grateful for today:

_____

Check the Feeling Wheel inside the front cover and list any emotion(s) you are feeling.

1.3 DAY 3: Developing Self-Confidence

|||||||||||||||||||||||||||||||||||||||||||||||||||||||||||||||||||||||||||||||||||||||||||||||||||||||||||||||||||||||||||||

☆ *"The most beautiful thing you can wear is confidence."*
  —Blake Lively

Practice for Today: Think about something that might be challenging today. How can you wear your confidence and show your abilities?

_____

_____

_____

_____

_____

_____

List one thing you're grateful for today:

_____

Check the Feeling Wheel inside the front cover and list any emotion(s) you are feeling.

1.3 DAY 4: Developing Self-Confidence

☆ *"When someone tells me 'no,' it doesn't mean I can't do it, it simply means I can't do it with them."* —Karen E. Quinones Miller

Practice for Today: What great undertaking needs to happen at your school? What do you need to gain more confidence in to lead this undertaking? How will you do this?

_____

_____

_____

_____

_____

_____

List one thing you're grateful for today:

_____

Check the Feeling Wheel inside the front cover and list any emotion(s) you are feeling.

1.3 DAY 5: Developing Self-Confidence

||||||||||||||||||||||||||||||||||||||||||||||||||||||||||||||||||||||||||||||||||||||||||||||||||||||||||||||||||||||

☆ *"Each time we face our fear, we gain strength, courage, and confidence in the doing."* —Theodore Roosevelt

Leadership Considerations: This week, you reflected on and practiced developing self-confidence. As you think more about this skill, consider these questions:

1. How does the degree of my self-confidence impact others? Where do I need to gain more self-confidence?

2. How can I lead my staff and students to develop their self-confidence?

3. Review all the notes you took this week and find your one best thought. Now go share your insight with somebody who might benefit from it.

Weekly Effort	1	2	3	4	5
	none	minimal	some	moderate	significant

Weekly Impact	1	2	3	4	5

Check the Feeling Wheel inside the front cover and list any emotion(s) you are feeling.

WEEK 1.4: Developing Self-Efficacy

Similar to self-confidence, self-efficacy is defined as the belief that one has in one's ability to succeed or reach a goal. It is a belief in your abilities to exert control and motivation over your behavior toward something aspirational. Self-efficacy is future-facing (compared to self-confidence, which is backward-facing) in that you believe you can accomplish a goal you set for yourself in the future. If you have a high sense of self-efficacy, you tend to set more ambitious goals and have higher degrees of motivation to succeed. With a high degree of self-efficacy, you also tend to take more risks, persist toward goals longer, and know how to advocate for yourself.

> **Self-efficacy is future-facing; self-confidence is backward-facing.**

In today's educational environment, you need to develop a high degree of self-efficacy in many new and complex areas. With complex change, more ambitious learning, technology, and a volatile environment, you need to develop a sense of efficacy to handle all that comes your way for the sake of your staff and students. Self-efficacy can develop from positive past experiences, learning from others, social persuasion through coaching and feedback, imagining success, and recognizing the physical and emotional states that alert you when facing a challenge.

This week we use quotes from Albert Bandura, the psychologist who developed the theory of self-efficacy, among others. As you explore your self-efficacy, reflect on why self-efficacy is critical to grow as a leader. We also want to point out that you might wish to move back and forth between this skill and the synergistic skills **2.1 Self-Motivation, 2.2 Goal-Setting and Productive Habits, and 2.6 Self-Discipline.**

1.4 DAY 1: Developing Self-Efficacy

☆ *"Self-belief does not necessarily ensure success, but self-disbelief assuredly spawns failure."* —Albert Bandura

Reflection for Today: As a school leader, where do you feel most self-efficacious? Where do you feel less self-efficacious, and how does this show up in your leadership?

_____

_____

_____

_____

_____

_____

List one thing you're grateful for today:

_____

Check the Feeling Wheel inside the front cover and list any emotion(s) you are feeling.

1.4 DAY 2: Developing Self-Efficacy

☆ *"Confront the dark parts of yourself, and work to banish them with illumination and forgiveness. Your willingness to wrestle with your demons will cause your angels to sing."*
—August Wilson

Reflection for Today: As a school leader, where and in what ways do you need to persist in your development of greater self-efficacy?

_____

_____

_____

_____

_____

List one thing you're grateful for today:

_____

Check the Feeling Wheel inside the front cover and list any emotion(s) you are feeling.

1.4 DAY 3: Developing Self-Efficacy

☆ *"Everything that happens to you is a reflection of what you believe about yourself. We cannot outperform our level of self-esteem. We cannot draw to ourselves more than we think we are worth."* —IIyanla Vanzant

Practice for Today: Think about to what or whom you want to draw closer. Decide how you might do that and try it.

_____

_____

_____

_____

_____

List one thing you're grateful for today:

_____

Check the Feeling Wheel inside the front cover and list any emotion(s) you are feeling.

1.4 DAY 4: Developing Self-Efficacy

☆ *"I really do believe that if you don't challenge yourself and risk failing, that it's not interesting."* —Julie Taymor

Practice for Today: Today, think about the most challenging task you need to accomplish today or in the very near future. Now plan out how you will challenge yourself to master this task.

_____

_____

_____

_____

_____

List one thing you're grateful for today:

_____

Check the Feeling Wheel inside the front cover and list any emotion(s) you are feeling.

1.4 DAY 5: Developing Self-Efficacy

 "People's beliefs about their abilities have a profound effect on these abilities. Ability is not a fixed property; there is a huge variability in how you perform." —Albert Bandura

Leadership Considerations: This week, you reflected on and practiced developing self-efficacy. As you think more about this skill, consider these questions:

1. How do the areas where you feel most self-efficacious impact others? How do the areas where you feel less self-efficacy impact others? What can you accept as a challenge?

2. How can you lead your staff and students to consider developing their self-efficacy? How can you use this content and your new understandings with your staff and students?

3. Review all the notes you took this week and find your one best thought. Now go share your insight with somebody who might benefit from it.

Weekly Effort	1	2	3	4	5
	none	minimal	some	moderate	significant

Weekly Impact	1	2	3	4	5

Check the Feeling Wheel inside the front cover and list any emotion(s) you are feeling.

Reflection and Action Planning

1. What do you see as the key ideas to continue to think and learn about in this module?

2. Are there any skills from the diagnostic or your initial practice attempts you want to keep working on? If you haven't done so already, add the skill to your action plan.

Module Effort	1	2	3	4	5
	none	minimal	some	moderate	significant

Module Impact	1	2	3	4	5

Check the Feeling Wheel inside the front cover and list any emotion(s) you are feeling.

MODULE 2: SELF-MANAGEMENT

||||||||||||||||||||||||||||||||||||||||||||||||||||||||||||||||||||||||||||||||||||||||||||||||||||||||||||||||

Self-management, as defined by CASEL, is the "abilit[y] to manage one's emotions, thoughts, and behaviors effectively in different situations and to achieve goals and aspirations" (CASEL, n.d.). This competency flows naturally from self-awareness; you have to be highly aware of your inner thoughts and emotions before you can manage them. If you feel as though you have not yet mastered self-awareness, you might choose to continue developing those skills before deciding to focus on self-management.

To get a glimpse into self-management, let's consider a composite example, selected from interviews with school leaders around the country, of a typical Monday morning. Afterward, we dissect the scenario in terms of self-management, in an attempt to link, concretely, self-management concepts to your daily experience and practice.

> Mr. Martinez, school leader at Blue Grove Middle School in suburban Kansas City, arrives at school at 6:30 a.m. Every day, he opens the doors to the community at 7:15 a.m., personally greeting families and students. This morning, Mr. Martinez picked up donuts for his staff and dropped them off in the staff room. He grabbed a glazed donut for himself and headed into his office.
>
> His desk, a mountain range of administrative piles, stretching from facilities plans to student discipline documentation, reflected Mr. Martinez's all too common harried work environment. Looking to prepare for a meeting later in the day regarding the progress of a particular student who'd recently suffered trauma in her home, Mr. Martinez spent 10 minutes moving papers around and searching through his inbox until he was able to find what he needed to review. The student's situation was extremely complex; and now, with just 25 minutes left before he had to welcome the community, Mr. Martinez was rapidly scanning his RTI team's observations and recommendations. None of the recommendations addressed how the school was going to meet the family's demands for a neuropsychological evaluation. Mr. Martinez felt his heart begin to race a bit, because he knew he would not have any more time to prepare for the meeting once the school day began.

As he continued to scan the documents, a staff member came into his office in tears. Mr. James, a second-year teacher who had been struggling, told Mr. Martinez he was not sure he could finish the year. While it was only October, the idea of losing a teacher so soon caused another wave of anxiety to crash over Mr. Martinez. Looking at the clock, which read 7:09 a.m., and glancing at the RTI team's incomplete documents and then at the tears streaming down Mr. James's face, Mr. Martinez found himself scolding Mr. James for barging in with this news and curtly asked him to come back at the end of the day. He pushed his chair from his desk, cursed about how his week was starting, and grabbed another donut from the staff room. He wondered whether or not he would make it through the year, too.

Research Basis for Self-Management

Unfortunately, this scenario is not a far-fetched one. Your role as a school leader is demonstrably the most demanding one on a school district's organization chart. This small example illustrates the nonstop, varied and complex situations that can bombard you. It is nearly inconceivable to imagine a school leader serving their community effectively without a significant degree of self-management.

Like many of these competencies, self-management is a combination of many different constructs and ideas in the psychological literature. One basis for self-management comes from self-regulation theory. In short, this theory suggests that self-regulation is guiding one's own thoughts, behaviors, and feelings to reach our goals. Because we as humans have many goals at once, we must manage or regulate our own motivation, development, and behavior within a network of multiple, interacting influences. Social psychologists who have studied self-management and self-regulation claim that it consists of four components: standards of desirable behavior, motivation to reach those standards, monitoring of situations and thoughts about those standards, and willpower (Muraven & Baumeister, 2000). Many psychologists also believe that willpower, or that ability to overcome one's urges, is a resource that can be expended during a day, making self-management more difficult.

Many discrete skills contribute to your overall capacity to self-manage effectively. These include

- Impulse control
- Stress management

- Self-discipline

- Self-motivation

- Goal setting

- Organizational skills

Let's take a quick look at each component of self-management to provide you with a simple, working understanding of each skill and why they matter to school leadership.

Impulse control refers to your ability to choose not to respond prematurely or without contemplating the future impact of a premature response to a given stimulus (Evenden, 1999). As an extreme example, choosing to fire a staff member because they expressed a political view in a team meeting with which you disagree would reflect a lack of impulse control, and most likely would lead to a lawsuit. A leader with impulse control would be able to take in the personally offensive perspective, process it, and find a productive, healthy, and legal means of addressing the issue (if the issue even persisted as a problem in the leader's mind once some time has passed). Impulse control matters for leaders because it prevents you from saying things you shouldn't and acting on urges that may not be in the best interest of your school's community.

Stress management is exactly what it sounds like: The use of strategies to reduce the toll your life's stresses—both your professional AND your personal stresses—take on your capacity to lead. A wide range of choices exist that can contribute to managing your stress, from meditation to exercise to vacation to effective prioritization. What is most important is that through self-awareness you calibrate your level of stress at any given time and then select strategies that appeal to you to manage that stress. As a leading source, the Mayo Clinic (2014) observes that failing to manage stress can lead to frightening health outcomes, including chest pain, headache, gastrointestinal complications, and sleep deprivation, to name only some of the consequences. Stress management matters for leaders because it helps you with your long-term health and well-being, both of which are necessary to lead a school effectively.

Self-discipline addresses your capacity to make good choices in furtherance of your stated goals. Do you find yourself wandering over to your inbox or YouTube when work becomes difficult or tedious? If so, you may need to work on developing your self-discipline. Similar to impulse control, self-discipline importantly includes a connection to goal achievement, as the American Psychological Association (APA, n.d.) notes in its rigorous second definition of the term. According to the APA, self-discipline is the "resolute adherence to a regimen or course of action in order to achieve one's goals." Self-discipline matters for leaders because it helps show the way for others and helps you meet your set goals.

Self-motivation describes your drive to achieve your goals. You can think of it as a fundamental drive in Maslow's Hierarchy of Needs. We humans are motivated to better ourselves and work our way up the ladder to achieve increasing levels of safety, satisfaction, and, ultimately, self-actualization (Motivation, n.d.). Each one of us has the power to influence our degree of self-motivation. If you lack motivation, it might be due to an ill-defined goal, or maybe you lack the confidence to persist in going after your goal. Whatever the explanation may be, recognize that there are no excuses: you can increase your self-motivation capacity (Motivation, n.d.). Self-motivation matters for leaders because it drives you and your school forward.

Goal setting is the essential SEL skill to master. It draws on other SEL stand-outs like self-awareness and aspects of self-management, such as self-discipline and self-motivation, while also directly contributing to influencing the all-important concept of self-efficacy. Leaders (all humans, in fact) who can set well-defined goals, monitor progress, experience success, and repeat this cycle will boost their perceived self-efficacy, supercharging the next goal setting cycle (Schunk, 1990). You could do worse than to focus your entire community on becoming excellent goal setters and monitors. Goal setting matters for leaders because it helps you grow as a person and model for staff and students how to improve continually.

Organizational skills, relative to the rest of this list, are more concrete ideas to understand, though they are no less important than any other skill. What's your workspace look like? Do you waste time sifting through folders on your desk or your computer trying to locate that needed resource? How's your time management? Are you able to stick to deadlines, or even better, set deadlines for yourself and meet them? Do you consider yourself a strong delegator, making time, and allocating your energy to the highest impact work? Such skills support your ability to deliver on and grow many of the other powers listed previously. Organizational skills matter for leaders because they help you save time and energy for more critical parts of your work.

Why Self-Management is Critical for School Leaders

It's not hard to see the through line connecting self-awareness to the discrete skills that comprise effective self-management. As a leader, if you are unable to manage your impulses and stress, discipline yourself to maintain focus on what is truly most important for your community, or set, monitor, and adjust goals, then your lack of self-management skills will significantly impact, and almost certainly be reflected in, your community's experience. The next time a staff member or student demonstrates a lack of self-management, ask yourself whether you truly have the higher moral ground or, perhaps, they are just being human. By applying self-awareness here, you'll also create an opportunity to uncover a need for more self-management development.

From the self-regulation theory presented earlier, there are numerous examples of where Mr. Martinez could improve his performance, and thus others' experiences, as a result of better self-management.

First, although the act of bringing staff breakfast is commendable, there are healthier options than donuts, which present an immediate challenge to both Mr. Martinez's and his staff's impulse control. The sugar rush those donuts will provide is short-lived and short-sighted and will not contribute to either Mr. Martinez or his team being their very best, especially at the start of the week. It would be better not to bring anything rather than food that will sap valuable energy in the form of impulse control. Mr. Martinez could also choose to bring a healthier choice, such as quality coffee or fruit, for his staff. Note, as well, that the donuts take a second toll on Mr. Martinez because he chooses to eat another one after his stress level rises significantly over just the first 45 minutes of his day. In this case, self-management is critical to stay healthy to handle the demands of the role.

Second, Mr. Martinez's desk, though likely not an outlier in terms of school leaders' desks across the country, nonetheless reflects a lack of self-management. As the school leader, the example Mr. Martinez sets will be internalized by others in the community as well. If Mr. Martinez cannot maintain an organized, orderly workspace, not only is he communicating that this is OK for his staff members, too, but he is also allowing himself to waste precious minutes having to search for critical documents. In this analysis, self-management is necessary to reduce the stress and be more efficient with your time.

Third, following the first donut, searching for the necessary documents, and then discovering that the documents are not up to his standards, Mr. Martinez begins to feel his stress level rising. In this example, he does not implement any kind of tool or routine to combat this feeling, and as that stress level rises, an emotional staff member enters his office. Mr. Martinez does not adjust to put himself into a position to successfully and supportively be present with the staff member. As a result, lacking stress management and self-discipline tools and practices, he finds himself unable to provide the strength the demoralized teacher needs from him. Mr. Martinez externalizes his shortcomings to his teacher, leaving his teacher feeling uncared for and of little importance to him. With a rapidly dwindling supply of energy and the day not even truly underway, Mr. Martinez succumbs to the second donut, despite knowing that he's making a wrong choice. In this case, self-management is necessary to provide emotional support to your staff.

There are several other examples of a lack of self-management in this scenario, but the point should be clear: Mr. Martinez is unable to be his best, both for himself and others, due in part to a lack of self-management.

Self-management is the engine that drives the representation and expression of so much of what SEL education and leadership prizes. It's secondary to self-awareness, but once you've developed an understanding of your strengths and weaknesses, self-management provides the behavior playbook necessary to advance every other aspect of your SEL practice significantly.

> Once you've developed an understanding of your strengths and weaknesses, self-management provides the behavior playbook necessary to advance every other aspect of your SEL practice significantly.

MODULE 2: SELF-MANAGEMENT

In this module you will learn more about Self-Management through

Week 2.1: Self-Motivation

Week 2.2: Goal Setting and Productive Habits

Week 2.3: Organizational Skills

Week 2.4: Impulse Control

Week 2.5: Stress Management

Week 2.6: Self-Discipline

WEEK 2.1: Self-Motivation

To become highly self-managed as a person and school leader, you must first understand what drives your day-to-day decisions. This internal drive is explicitly known as *intrinsic* or *self-motivation*. Your self-motivation is how you express your tendencies or needs without any external influence or constraints. These are the things you do because they are exciting or satisfying to you; they have become internalized. For instance, spending lots of time interacting with students versus time in your office is an internal or self-motivated drive.

Self-motivation is related strongly to a popular theory called *self-determination theory*. This theory states that self-determination is a feature of all human beings and that all people have innate psychological needs that motivate them toward optimal growth and functioning. These needs include

- competence, or the feeling that you are good at something, so you choose to continue;

- relatedness, or the impression that you want to connect to and interact with others; and

- autonomy, or the drive that you want to be the cause of success in your own life (Ryan & Deci, 2017).

Each of these needs is often subconscious to us and performs in the background to drive our behaviors.

This week as you lead your school and complete your myriad tasks, consider which you are most and least motivated to do. Then consider the degree of competence, relatedness, or autonomy you have with each. We also want to point out that you might wish to move back and forth between this skill and the synergistic skills **1.1 Developing Accurate Self-Perception, 1.3 Developing Self-Confidence, and 1.4 Developing Self-Efficacy.**

2.1 DAY 1: Self-Motivation

⟨☆⟩ *"Sometimes later becomes never so do it now."*
—Kanka Bisht

Reflection for Today: What is something you have been putting off for a long time? Is this because you don't feel competent in doing it, it may ruin a relationship, or somebody else is making you do it? Write about that below.

_____

_____

_____

_____

_____

List one thing you're grateful for today:

_____

Check the Feeling Wheel inside the front cover and list any emotion(s) you are feeling.

2.1 DAY 2: Self-Motivation

☆ *"You don't need a fan club to achieve your goals.*
Be your own motivation." —Mama Zara

Reflection for Today: Remind yourself today of your personal and professional goals. What do you need to pay more attention to or get back to doing to achieve those goals?

_____

_____

_____

_____

_____

List one thing you're grateful for today:

_____

Check the Feeling Wheel inside the front cover and list any emotion(s) you are feeling.

2.1 DAY 3: Self-Motivation

☆ *"Strive for continuous improvement instead of perfection."* —Kim Collins

Practice for Today: Think about a leadership practice you have been developing. How can you move even closer to competence by practicing this skill? For today, practice that skill, even if only a tiny bit.

_____

_____

_____

_____

_____

List one thing you're grateful for today:

_____

Check the Feeling Wheel inside the front cover and list any emotion(s) you are feeling.

2.1 DAY 4: Self-Motivation

☆ *"You must have a level of discontent to feel the urge to want to grow."* —Idowu Koyenikan

Practice for Today: As you look at your leadership practice, with which aspect of it do you feel most discontent? How can you use your sense of autonomy to grow in this area? For today, practice that skill.

_____

_____

_____

_____

_____

List one thing you're grateful for today:

_____

Check the Feeling Wheel inside the front cover and list any emotion(s) you are feeling.

21 DAY 5: Self-Motivation

☆ *"Your motivations are your own. You must master them if you want to do great work."* —Brian Knapp

Leadership Considerations: This week you reflected on and practiced developing self-motivation. As you think more about this skill, consider these questions:

1. Which of the three needs of competency, relatedness, or autonomy drives most of your self-motivation? How do those needs impact others? Is there a need that seems to be more of a challenge for you? Why?

2. How can you lead your staff and students to consider developing their self-motivation using these three needs?

3. Review all the notes you took this week and find your one best thought. Now go share your insight with somebody who might benefit from it.

Weekly Effort	1	2	3	4	5
	none	minimal	some	moderate	significant

Weekly Impact	1	2	3	4	5

Check the Feeling Wheel inside the front cover and list any emotion(s) you are feeling.

WEEK 2.2: Goal Setting and Productive Habits

Another skill that helps leaders increase their capacity to self-manage is the science and art of goal setting and developing productive habits. The science is pretty clear around goal setting. Goals are a foundational part of achievement and success for anyone. Like self-determination theory, goals are most potent when they align well with your interests, values, and motivations. When goals are imposed on you, you may comply, but the goal's success is not as meaningful or powerful.

You can set goals in any area. You may want to focus on the relational aspect of your leadership or spend more time in classrooms giving feedback. You may have a long-term goal of getting an advanced degree or moving into a different position. No matter the actual target, goal setting becomes most potent when you feel you can choose or self-determine your own goals or possess an internal locus of control to complete those goals.

However, the art of goal setting often gets overlooked. As a successful leader, you have made progress in your life and career, and you continue to make steady progress toward your goals in a linear fashion. Yet we all can become frustrated when we don't make progress during the first days, weeks, or months after setting a goal. Goals do not happen by themselves but require the internal drive and systems that align your habits with your goals. Your goals are the lagging measures of your habits (Clear, 2019). Systems and habits could include a weekly and daily time management system, a method for sharing documents, or a meeting planning system. Creating sound systems and habits are the secret to reaching your goals. It is your ongoing commitment to creating a system that works for you that determines if you ever meet your goals.

This week, you'll explore the quality of your goal setting and habit-forming practices. We also want to point out that you might wish to move back and forth between this skill and the synergistic skills **1.1 Developing Accurate Self-Perception, 1.2 Strengths of Emotions, and 1.4 Developing Self-Efficacy.**

2.2 DAY 1: Goal Setting and Productive Habits

☆ *"The purpose of setting goals is to win the game. The purpose of building systems is to continue playing the game."* —James Clear

Reflection for Today: As you think about your goals, are you trying to win the game (i.e., just get through every day)? Or are you trying to continue playing the game by developing goals and productivity habits?

_____

_____

_____

_____

List one thing you're grateful for today:

_____

Check the Feeling Wheel inside the front cover and list any emotion(s) you are feeling.

2.2 DAY 2: Goal Setting and Productive Habits

☆ *"When it is obvious that the goals cannot be reached, don't adjust the goals, adjust the action steps."*
—Confucius

Reflection for Today: As you think about your personal goals, what systems do you have in place to reach these goals? Are they supportive enough to help you reach your goals?

_____

_____

_____

_____

List one thing you're grateful for today:

_____

Check the Feeling Wheel inside the front cover and list any emotion(s) you are feeling.

22 DAY 3: Goal Setting and Productive Habits

☆ *"If the quality and quantity of continuous effort toward goals matters as much as I think it does, we may actually get more productive, not less, as we get older—even if we can't pull all-nighters like we used to."* —Angela Duckworth

Practice for Today: Think about any personal goal you have set for yourself recently. What are the repeatable steps that will create a habit that will help you reach your goal? Start today.

List one thing you're grateful for today:

Check the Feeling Wheel inside the front cover and list any emotion(s) you are feeling.

2.2 DAY 4: Goal Setting and Productive Habits

☆ *"Goals are harmful unless they guide you to make specific behaviors easier to do. Don't focus your motivation on doing Behavior X. Instead, focus on making Behavior X easier to do."* —B. J. Fogg

Practice for Today: Think about a behavior that you have been meaning to change, like less time on email or more time with students. Now think about how you could make that behavior easier to achieve through creating a different habit. Try it today.

_____

_____

_____

_____

List one thing you're grateful for today:

_____

Check the Feeling Wheel inside the front cover and list any emotion(s) you are feeling.

2.2 DAY 5: Goal Setting and Productive Habits

☆ *"Our goals can only be reached through a vehicle of a plan, in which we must fervently believe, and upon which we must vigorously act. There is no other route to success."* —Pablo Picasso

Leadership Considerations: This week you reflected on and practiced goal setting and developing productive habits. As you think more about this skill, consider these questions:

1. Have you set challenging goals for yourself, and if so, have you designed and created powerful supporting habits to reach these goals?

2. How can you lead your staff and students to consider developing their own self-determined goals and powerful supporting habits to achieve these goals?

3. Review all the notes you took this week and find your one best thought. Now go share your insight with somebody who might benefit from it.

Weekly Effort	1	2	3	4	5
	none	minimal	some	moderate	significant

Weekly Impact	1	2	3	4	5

Check the Feeling Wheel inside the front cover and list any emotion(s) you are feeling.

WEEK 2.3: Organizational Skills

Simply stated, to be self-managed is to possess and use a variety of organizational skills. Today's schools are busy and sometimes chaotic places, requiring school leaders to develop and use organizational systems and processes to manage their time, attention, and energy. Without these systems, school leaders get pulled in many different directions, which can sap the energy and vitality needed for the work of leading schools.

While there are many systems and processes to help school leaders organize themselves, at a minimum, we recommend that effective school leaders develop systems to organize and protect

- Your time daily, weekly, and yearly

- Your energy daily, weekly, and yearly

- Student or personnel situations that occur in school

- Specific roles and functions of your job

- Flows of information and knowledge

This week you'll focus on how robust systems and processes can help create better workflows and help you better manage the flow of energy and information necessary for leading. We also want to point out that you might wish to move back and forth between this skill and the synergistic skill **2.5 Stress Management.**

2.3 DAY 1: Organizational Skills

☆ *"Managing your time without setting priorities is like shooting randomly and calling whatever you hit the target."* —Peter Turla

Reflection for Today: Think about your time management system. How do you set your monthly, weekly, and daily priorities, and how do you know if it is working?

_____

_____

_____

_____

_____

List one thing you're grateful for today:

_____

Check the Feeling Wheel inside the front cover and list any emotion(s) you are feeling.

2.3 DAY 2: Organizational Skills

☆ *"The space in which we live should be for the person we are becoming now, not for the person we were in the past."* —Marie Kondo

Reflection for Today: Think about your current workspace and how you might redesign it for the leader you want to become.

_____

_____

_____

_____

_____

List one thing you're grateful for today:

_____

Check the Feeling Wheel inside the front cover and list any emotion(s) you are feeling.

23 DAY 3: Organizational Skills

☆ *"Organizing isn't about perfection; it's about efficiency, reducing stress and clutter, saving time and money and improving your overall quality of life."* —Christina Scalise

Practice for Today: Start simple. Clean the clutter on your desk and create a more simplified way to manage the flow of paper. Or do the same with your email inbox.

List one thing you're grateful for today:

Check the Feeling Wheel inside the front cover and list any emotion(s) you are feeling.

23 DAY 4: Organizational Skills

☆ *"For every minute spent organizing, an hour is earned."* —Benjamin Franklin

Practice for Today: Think about when you have the most energy during the day. Now think about your three most important tasks that need to get done today. Do these during your high energy time and make this a habit.

_____

_____

_____

_____

_____

List one thing you're grateful for today:

_____

Check the Feeling Wheel inside the front cover and list any emotion(s) you are feeling.

2.3 DAY 5: Organizational Skills

||||||||||||||||||||||||||||||||||||||||||||||||||||||||||||||||||||||||||||||||||||||||||||||||||||||||||||||||||||||||||||||||||

☆ *"Being organized is all about the ABC's: Awareness and Action, Balance and Beliefs, Choices and Consistency."* —Tanya Allason

Leadership Considerations: This week you reflected on and started practicing organizational skills. As you think more about this skill, consider these questions:

1. Do you have productive systems and processes to manage your time, energy, situations, specific tasks, and information?

2. How can you lead your staff and students to consider developing their systems and processes for organizing?

3. Review all the notes you took this week and find your one best thought. Now go share your insight with somebody who might benefit from it.

Weekly Effort	1	2	3	4	5
	none	minimal	some	moderate	significant
Weekly Impact	1	2	3	4	5

Check the Feeling Wheel inside the front cover and list any emotion(s) you are feeling.

WEEK 2.4: Impulse Control

|||||||||||||||||||||||||||||||||||||||||||||||||||||||||||||||||||||||||||||||||||||||||||||||||||||||||||||||||||||||||||||||||||||||||||||

If you've never watched a version of the (in)famous Marshmallow Test, take a moment to look it up in a search engine. The experiment, intended to connect a child's ability to delay gratification with higher academic outcomes later on in life, has been debunked in recent history. Still, it provides an entertaining way to shine a light on our impulse control, nonetheless. How capable are you of delaying your impulses in your personal and professional life? Are you a one-marshmallow or two-marshmallow person?

This week, you'll focus on impulse control. As a leader, in the heat of extremely complex moments at school, your capacity to demonstrate impulse control and to seek understanding over asserting your power is essential. Like all valuable skills, impulse control is difficult to develop, requires consistent practice, and will yield outsized results to your community and you after mastery. We also want to point out that you might wish to move back and forth between this skill and the synergistic skill **1.4 Developing Self-Efficacy.**

24 DAY 1: Impulse Control

☆ *"Ultimately, the only power to which man should aspire is that which he exercises over himself."*
—Elie Wiesel

Reflection for Today: Pay attention to the frequency with which you attempt to exercise power over others today vs. the rate you attempt to control your impulses. Is your typical desire to try to exercise authority or to listen deeply?

List one thing you're grateful for today:

Check the Feeling Wheel inside the front cover and list any emotion(s) you are feeling.

24 DAY 2: Impulse Control

☆ *"You may not control all of the events that happen to you, but you can decide not to be reduced by them."*
—Maya Angelou

Reflection for Today: In general, do you find yourself overwhelmed by your day's events, or are you able to maintain perspective and control while engaging with the immense challenges of your job? How might impulse control relate to your feelings?

_____

_____

_____

_____

List one thing you're grateful for today:

_____

Check the Feeling Wheel inside the front cover and list any emotion(s) you are feeling.

Module 2

24 DAY 3: Impulse Control

 "It takes more to abstain than to err, more to avoid mistakes than to make mistakes; but the good thing is that it gets better with practice."
—Innocent Mwatsikesimbe

Practice for Today: Focus on abstaining from allowing your impulses to rule you today. When a strong feeling or emotion begins to surface, recognize it, ignore it, and focus on understanding why this feeling is coming up. Take heart in knowing that a more considered response is almost certainly going to be better than an impulse-driven response.

List one thing you're grateful for today:

Check the Feeling Wheel inside the front cover and list any emotion(s) you are feeling.

2.4 DAY 4: Impulse Control

 "Not to have control over the senses is like sailing in a rudderless ship, bound to break to pieces on coming in contact with the very first rock."
—Mahatma Gandhi

Practice for Today: Pay attention to the events and people who seem to most contribute to a decrease in your impulse control. How might you be able to change your environment to support your ability to maintain impulse control when you find yourself challenged?

List one thing you're grateful for today:

Check the Feeling Wheel inside the front cover and list any emotion(s) you are feeling.

24 DAY 5: Impulse Control

☆ *"Some people plan on being disciplined as soon as they achieve something that cannot be achieved without discipline."* —Mokokoma Mokhonoana

Leadership Considerations: This week, you reflected on the status and quality of your impulse control. As you think more about this skill, consider these questions:

1. What routines and rituals, *outside of school*, do you have in place that support your consistent development of impulse control?

2. What might be the most straightforward and scalable impulse control practice you could reasonably introduce and support your staff in adopting at school?

3. Review all the notes you took this week and find your one best thought. Now go share your insight with somebody who might benefit from it.

Weekly Effort	1	2	3	4	5
	none	minimal	some	moderate	significant
Weekly Impact	1	2	3	4	5

Check the Feeling Wheel inside the front cover and list any emotion(s) you are feeling.

WEEK 2.5: Stress Management

Stress management is an entire industry unto itself, and with good reason. Stress kills.

You know full well how stressful your job is, and unfortunately, the conditions that contribute to your stress are unlikely to change any time soon. However, you can accept that reality while also proactively taking steps to manage the stress that comes with leading your community.

This week, you will focus on developing a more robust stress management practice. In your role, as is the case for so many of the characteristics of a leader, how you manage your stress will directly impact those with whom you work and the students you serve. If you are not actively taking steps to manage the stress in your life and work, now is the time to start.

We also want to point out that you might wish to move back and forth between this skill and the synergistic skill **1.1 Developing Accurate Self-Perception.**

25 DAY 1: Stress Management

☆ *"Don't believe every worried thought you have.*
Worried thoughts are notoriously inaccurate."
—Renee Jain

Reflection for Today: Do you typically pay attention to your worries? What is worrying you most at this moment? Observe whether or not you even provide yourself with a brief moment to pause to consider the truth of your fears.

List one thing you're grateful for today:

Check the Feeling Wheel inside the front cover and list any emotion(s) you are feeling.

2.5 DAY 2: Stress Management

☆ *"It is not a daily increase, but a daily decrease. Hack away at the inessentials."* —Bruce Lee

Reflection for Today: Pay attention to what most demands your time today and where you give most of your time. Is everything essential? What might you be able to remove from your life that seems important, but is actually causing you excess stress?

List one thing you're grateful for today:

Check the Feeling Wheel inside the front cover and list any emotion(s) you are feeling.

25 DAY 3: Stress Management

☆ *"If the problem can be solved, why worry? If the problem cannot be solved, worrying will do you no good."* —Buddha

Practice for Today: Your energy, as the leader of your community, is a very precious and scarce commodity. Today, focus on intentionally making the best possible decisions about how and when you invest that energy in problems that can be solved. Stressing out is unlikely to contribute to your efforts to improve your community's well-being.

List one thing you're grateful for today:

Check the Feeling Wheel inside the front cover and list any emotion(s) you are feeling.

2.5 DAY 4: Stress Management

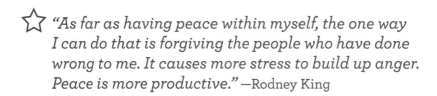

☆ *"As far as having peace within myself, the one way
I can do that is forgiving the people who have done
wrong to me. It causes more stress to build up anger.
Peace is more productive."* —Rodney King

Practice for Today: As you go through your day, be intentional about recognizing stress-inducing situations and plan on turning them into energizing opportunities rather than deflating problems. Plan to see your stressors as opportunities rather than setbacks.

_____

_____

_____

_____

List one thing you're grateful for today:

_____

Check the Feeling Wheel inside the front cover and list any emotion(s) you are feeling.

25 DAY 5: Stress Management

 "Stress ... believes that everything is an emergency."
—Natalie Goldberg

Leadership Considerations: As a leader, if you're stressed, the chances are high that your community will be as well. As you think more about this skill, consider these questions:

1. How might you unintentionally contribute to your community's stress level, and how might you minimize that impact?

2. Are there any trends you can identify related to your stress levels and that of your community? How might you change your practice to anticipate and mitigate any stress level trends?

3. Review all the notes you took this week and find your one best thought. Now go share your insight with somebody who might benefit from it.

Weekly Effort	1	2	3	4	5
	none	minimal	some	moderate	significant

Weekly Impact	1	2	3	4	5

Check the Feeling Wheel inside the front cover and list any emotion(s) you are feeling.

WEEK 2.6: Self-Discipline

Impulse control, or self-control, as you saw earlier, is the ability to control your inner urges so as to avoid making bad choices. Self-discipline, this week's focus, is the capacity to do what is necessary to make good choices.

Take a quick inventory of your current state of self-discipline. How often do you choose to do what is both necessary and hard? When was the last time you attempted and failed at something that scared you? When was the last time you took a cold shower or fasted (notoriously challenging tasks that require a considerable level of self-discipline for most of us)?

Self-discipline is at the heart of this book. Without developing your self-discipline, your potential to lead your community to success is mitigated, at best, and nullified entirely at worst.

This week, you'll focus on your self-discipline, how to improve it, and why it is so vital to your leadership practice. We also want to point out that you might wish to move back and forth between this skill and the synergistic skills **1.1 Developing Accurate Self-Perception and 1.2 Strengths of Emotions.**

26 DAY 1: Self-Discipline

☆ *"I learned to discipline myself to do things I didn't want to do."* —James Edward Olmos

Reflection for Today: Think about how many parts of your day you experience as things you do not want to do and how you respond to them. Do you find it hard to persist through the work, or do you find that you have the discipline necessary to push through your resistance?

List one thing you're grateful for today:

Check the Feeling Wheel inside the front cover and list any emotion(s) you are feeling.

26 DAY 2: Self-Discipline

☆ *"I value self-discipline, but creating systems that make it next to impossible to misbehave is more reliable than self-control."* —Tim Ferriss

Reflection for Today: As your day goes on, your willpower likely decreases. What systems, tools, or routines might you create to help you when your self-discipline is low?

List one thing you're grateful for today:

Check the Feeling Wheel inside the front cover and list any emotion(s) you are feeling.

2.6 DAY 3: Self-Discipline

||||||||||||||||||||||||||||||||||||||||||||||||||||||||||||||||||||||||||||||||||||||||||||||||||||||||||||||||||||||||||||||||

☆ *"You don't make progress by standing on the sidelines whimpering and complaining. You make progress by implementing ideas."* —Shirley Chisolm

Practice for Today: Identify a source of "whimpering and complaining" in your professional life and pledge the discipline to remove it from your day, forever, or pledge the discipline to transform it into a source of inspiration and energy.

_____

_____

_____

_____

_____

List one thing you're grateful for today:

_____

Check the Feeling Wheel inside the front cover and list any emotion(s) you are feeling.

2.6 DAY 4: Self-Discipline

☆ *"Most of us aren't defeated in one decisive battle. We are defeated one tiny, seemingly insignificant surrender at a time that chips away at who we should really be."*
—Jocko Wilink

Practice for Today: Notice any small moments when you feel as though you are about to surrender, to give in to the easy path, to the lack of energy, to the opportunity to procrastinate. What do you observe when these moments arise? Practice regenerating your self-discipline in the moment.

_____

_____

_____

List one thing you're grateful for today:

_____

Check the Feeling Wheel inside the front cover and list any emotion(s) you are feeling.

26 DAY 5: Self-Discipline

☆ *The time is always right to do what is right."*
—Martin Luther King, Jr.

Leadership Considerations: The self-discipline you manifest as a school leader impacts everything that your community experiences. Without self-discipline, you cannot effectively lead your community. As you think more about this skill, consider these questions:

1. What hard, right, and necessary action have you been putting off for yourself and/or others? How might you get started on it, even in a small way, today?

2. How might increased community self-discipline contribute to better serving students? When do you intend to begin leading your community to do that thing?

3. Review all the notes you took this week and find your one best thought. Now go share your insight with somebody who might benefit from it.

Weekly Effort	1	2	3	4	5
	none	minimal	some	moderate	significant

Weekly Impact	1	2	3	4	5

Check the Feeling Wheel inside the front cover and list any emotion(s) you are feeling.

MODULE TWO

Reflection and Action Planning

1. What do you see as the key ideas to continue to think and learn about in this module?

2. Are there any skills from the diagnostic or your initial practice attempts you want to keep working on? If you haven't done so already, add the skill to your action plan.

Module Effort	1	2	3	4	5
	none	minimal	some	moderate	significant

Module Impact	1	2	3	4	5

Check the Feeling Wheel inside the front cover and list any emotion(s) you are feeling.

MODULE 3: SOCIAL AWARENESS

Social awareness, the focus for this module, is the sister topic to self-awareness, which we discussed in Module 1. Whereas self-awareness calls you to look inward to understand your strengths, perspectives, emotions, and needs, social awareness pushes you to look outward to learn about others, their views, and their feelings and needs. More specifically, CASEL (n.d.) defines social awareness as "[t]he abilities to understand the perspectives of and empathize with others, including those from diverse backgrounds, cultures, and contexts. This includes the capacities to feel compassion for others, understand broader historical and social norms for behavior in social settings, and recognize family, school, and community resources and supports."

As in other modules, with this brief definition in mind, now examine the following scenario depicting a busy school leader's morning. Consider all the situations in which this school leader must be socially aware and how her day may be like yours. Following the case study, we take a very brief look at the social awareness research base and connect the case study to the research to help inform your social awareness practice.

Ms. Bilal began her day at 6:30 a.m. She polished the agenda for her staff meeting scheduled later that morning, ensuring she would not waste her staff's precious time. She also designed the agenda to involve other staff leaders' talents, especially those who were particularly skilled at engaging faculty who were not exactly early morning people.

A critical agenda item included addressing a recent grading issue: Some parents had complained that boys seemed to receive higher grades than girls in some of the schools' classrooms. Ms. Bilal jotted a few notes on how to address the grading issue. Still, she was mindful that if she brought a seemingly fully developed solution to the meeting, her staff would likely disengage from any problem-solving exercises. On the other hand, she knew that she needed to provide just enough philosophical guidance and framing questions for the staff to consider so that the typically loudest voices in the room would not be able to dominate the conversation. Feeling prepared to facilitate the staff meeting, Ms. Bilal shared digital copies of the agenda and closed her laptop.

Before the staff meeting, Ms. Bilal had her first appointment at 7:15 a.m. with Mrs. Ruiz and her daughter Melissa. A 10th grader and typically a conscientious student, Melissa already had multiple absences and discipline referrals early in the semester. After the last incident, Ms. Bilal informed Melissa that she was required to bring in her mother before Melissa could return to school, leading to this morning's meeting.

After the initial greetings, Ms. Bilal began by asking why Melissa's attendance patterns had changed. Mrs. Ruiz explained that her husband left the family over the summer, causing Mrs. Ruiz to rely more on Melissa to care for her other three children. Moreover, Mrs. Ruiz recently lost her job, requiring Melissa to find work at a local fast-food restaurant to help the family. Through tears, Melissa confided that she was exhausted and overwhelmed and some days it was just easier to stay home in bed than try to hold on to dreams of college.

At 7:45 a.m., amid her conference with the Ruizes, Ms. Bilal's assistant reminded her that the staff meeting was ready to begin. Ms. Jones told Mrs. Ruiz and Melissa that she would like them to stay to talk to one of the counselors regarding ways to handle stress and to develop a plan to keep Melissa in school. The Ruizes accepted Ms. Bilal's offer of a hug to end the meeting, and Ms. Bilal gathered her staff meeting notes and escorted the Ruizes to the counselor's office.

As she walked to the library, Ms. Bilal practiced her meeting opening in her head and anticipated the possible push back she might get from some of her staff. She walked past groups of students gathered in the halls and greeted them warmly. Her goal as a school leader was to make every student feel like they belonged and were part of the school family. She saw a student she needed to talk to who had used a derogatory term and made a mental note to find him after her meeting.

As she entered the library at 7:50, Ms. Bilal reminded herself to start with positive energy and affirmations to create an engaging and welcoming environment. She asked for everyone's attention, smiled, and offered congratulations to a few teachers for meeting student needs and extra effort over the past week. Ms. Bilal then launched into framing the perception of unfair grading that families had raised and handed out her guiding questions as she broke her staff into discussion groups.

(Continued)

(Continued)

As teachers broke off into their groups, her phone buzzed. Her secretary informed her that a teacher had called in sick and there were no subs available.

At 8:15, Ms. Bilal called her staff back from their breakout groups and asked for brief comments. A veteran teacher responded that he thought parents had started to run the school and always ended up with what they wanted. Another teacher reported that her group agreed with families, which gave rise to surprise and groans from some of the other staff members. Knowing she only had a few minutes, Ms. Bilal could not meaningfully extend the conversation. Still, she thanked the teachers for their analysis and comments and reminded the whole staff that, above all else, grades needed to be meaningful and accurately reflect student achievement. She then reminded them to look at the weekly organizer regarding logistics for the week and released the staff in the usual way she ended meetings: "I appreciate you and thank you for your efforts."

At 8:20 a.m., as Ms. Bilal was gathering the notes from the teachers' tables for later analysis, a group of teachers who had stayed behind approached her. Immediately, she recognized some anger on their faces, placing her into a somewhat defensive mode. One teacher reported that she had heard their school might be losing teachers next year because of a decrease in enrollment, which meant larger class sizes. Ms. Bilal took a deep breath and reminded them that budgeting had just started and she would keep them updated.

Ms. Bilal then walked out of the library at 8:30 a.m. to start her day.

In this brief scenario, every situation encountered by Ms. Bilal required different levels of social awareness. From individuals to groups, you are likely well aware of the need to employ social awareness constantly. In one sense, we might say that being socially aware is your primary concern as a school leader. You have a social responsibility to your students and the adults who work in your building, the families, and others with whom you work. You are at the nexus of a complex social ecosystem that, in genuine ways, is only as strong as your social awareness skills.

Research Basis on Social Awareness

Social awareness is woven into our DNA; it speaks to our very capacity to live. Thousands of years ago, as our ancestors worked in tribes to survive, their brains developed into pattern-seeking machines watching and learning from the environment and each other. Our brains' very design and development make us prone to connect socially with others for survival, understanding, love, and trust. Our interpersonal radar has developed through many generations and helps us navigate all social situations. We are, in short, wired to connect (Goleman, 2006).

Like the other CASEL competencies, social awareness has a long and ever-evolving research basis that lets you understand the nature of this skill set. Simply put, our brains are regulated by those we spend the most time with, and the more connected you are with others emotionally, the greater the "mutual force" (Goleman, 2006). Anytime you are in the presence of one or more people, you involuntarily form a type of neural linkup that allows your brain to affect the other person's brain. As you enter a room and your brain connects with others', your emotions are primed and inform your body and regulate your biological systems. Social neuroscience finds that better relationships have a beneficial impact on the group and your health. Poor connections can have a detrimental effect on groups and health. In essence, our brains have evolved to be highly attuned to one another and to be aware of our relationships and be mindful of ourselves in our relationships (Feldman Barret, 2019)

With that brief research basis in mind, let's take a closer look at the components of social awareness. Here are four distinct aspects of social awareness that you'll want to practice:

- Perspective taking

- Empathy

- Appreciating diversity

- Respect for others

In the case study, there are numerous examples of Ms. Bilal's use of social awareness skills. For example, when planning out her staff meeting agenda, Ms. Bilal used perspective taking to anticipate how individual members of her staff might respond. When she met with Mrs. Ruiz and her daughter, it would have been easy to adhere to the hard and fast attendance rules, but instead she used empathy to understand the situation and maintain focus on supporting, not punishing, the

Ruizes. She also recognized and appreciated the diversity of experience the Ruizes lived, acknowledged their situation, and did not impose any solutions on them beyond connecting the Ruizes to a counselor to increase the school's support. In the staff meeting, by creating space for analysis of the grading issue and teacher voices, Ms. Bilal demonstrated respect for others and their professionalism. She also took perspective, empathized, and showed respect for others when she met with the small group at the end of the staff meeting.

In essence, social awareness is about how well you understand others, events, and situations and how, as a leader, you work to regulate interactions with others.

Why Social Awareness is Critical for School Leaders

Although all the social-emotional competencies are important for your success as a leader, social awareness may be the one by which you face the most scrutiny. Without social sensitivity for others, social insight on situations, and social communication, leading schools effectively becomes an impossible task. All paths to student achievement are gated by the quality of relationships between students, families, teachers, and your school's culture with you. Every minute you invest in developing your social awareness is a minute very well spent.

As a school leader, whether in a formal or informal capacity, you have a responsibility to create positive relationships and positive environments for your school community. Group dynamics and the health of others depend on it. A fundamental way to do this is through developing your social awareness. Social awareness is ultimately about the ability to interpret a social environment accurately, infer the emotions of others in that environment, and decide how to act, talk, and relate to others in that environment. Good social awareness emanates from good self-awareness (Module 1) and self-management (Module 2).

> As a school leader, whether in a formal or informal capacity, you have a responsibility to create positive relationships and positive environments for your school community.

So as you work through the skills in this module, consider what emotional signals you may be sending to others and how well you are reading social situations in your everyday duties.

MODULE 3: SOCIAL AWARENESS

In this module you will learn more about Social Awareness through

Week 3.1: Perspective Taking

Week 3.2: Empathy

Week 3.3: Appreciating Diversity

Week 3.4: Respect for Others

WEEK 3.1: Perspective Taking

Perspective taking is the foundational skill of social awareness, and it requires you to consider another person's point of view. This skill mirrors the proverbial idea of walking in another's shoes first before offering your own opinion. Since education is not an exact science in many respects, there will be numerous issues and problems that can be solved from many different perspectives. The mindset of excellent leaders seeks not to be right, but to listen and to hear others. Multiple and diverse perspectives are far more likely to yield productive responses to any complex situation you face.

> **The mindset of excellent leaders seeks not to be right, but to listen and to hear others.**

Perspective taking, however, does not quickly develop in most leaders. You advance as a leader based on your ideas and how you advocate for them. To develop your perspective-taking skill, you need to suspend your thoughts and opinions and consider how somebody else will experience or perceive a situation. You also need to consider how the thoughts, feelings, and attitudes of that person might enter the situation. Further, this skill requires that you understand the conditions in which you need to take different perspectives. In some circumstances, this may require that you prepare upfront, anticipating when different perspectives might emerge. In all cases, however, perspective taking requires deep and intentional listening to hear and honestly see others' truths.

This week you'll focus on the social awareness skill of perspective taking. As you think about this skill, consider the number of situations in which somebody offers a different perspective to yours, how easily you accept a different perspective, and how you manage these differences.

We also want to point out that you might wish to move back and forth between this skill and the synergistic skills **4.1 Communication, 4.2 Social Engagement, and 4.3 Relationship Building.**

3.1 DAY 1: Perspective Taking

☆ *"To change ourselves effectively, we first had to change our perceptions."* —Stephen R. Covey

Reflection for Today: In general, how easy or hard is it for you to change your perceptions of people, situations, or events? What allows you to or prevents you from changing your perceptions?

List one thing you're grateful for today:

Check the Feeling Wheel inside the front cover and list any emotion(s) you are feeling.

Module 3

3.1 DAY 2: Perspective Taking

⭐ *"Everything that irritates us about others can lead us to an understanding of ourselves."* —Carl Jung

Reflection for Today: Think about someone in your community who has a perspective that irritates you. What about their perspective is irritating? Are there any insights you can draw about yourself after thinking about why this person's perspective irritates you?

List one thing you're grateful for today:

Check the Feeling Wheel inside the front cover and list any emotion(s) you are feeling.

3.1 DAY 3: Perspective Taking

☆ *"In this treacherous world nothing is the truth nor a lie. Everything depends on the color of the crystal through which one sees it."* —Pedro Calderón de la Barca

Practice for Today: As you work with others today, try to identify and accept as valid, as quickly as possible, a perspective or opinion that is significantly different from your own on the subject at hand.

List one thing you're grateful for today:

Check the Feeling Wheel inside the front cover and list any emotion(s) you are feeling.

3.1 DAY 4: Perspective Taking

☆ *"The simple truth is that truth does not exist, it all depends on a person's point of view."* —Laura Esquivel

Practice for Today: Try to experience other people's perspectives today as if they were your own. Assume positive intent from others, and see how your thoughts and feelings might change by adopting someone else's perspective as your own.

List one thing you're grateful for today:

Check the Feeling Wheel inside the front cover and list any emotion(s) you are feeling.

3.1 DAY 5: Perspective Taking

☆ *"Loving people live in a loving world. Hostile people live in a hostile world. Same world."* —Wayne W. Dyer

Leadership Considerations: This week, you reflected on and practiced perspective taking. As you think more about this skill, consider these questions:

1. If you become good at taking different perspectives, what would you gain? What would you lose? What would your staff and students gain or lose?

2. Think about a situation or a person. Is there another perspective you could take to view that situation or person? How might that new perspective change how you think about it or them?"

3. Review all the notes you took this week and find your one best thought. Now go share your insight with somebody who might benefit from it.

Weekly Effort	1	2	3	4	5
	none	minimal	some	moderate	significant

Weekly Impact	1	2	3	4	5

Check the Feeling Wheel inside the front cover and list any emotion(s) you are feeling.

WEEK 3.2: Empathy

Empathy, another form of perspective taking, asks you to step outside of yourself. Notably, an essential aspect of improving your skill as a leader is a prompt to leave yourself behind. Yet, despite the paradox, empathy exercises ultimately seek to contribute to your growth by providing you with others' data—their words, emotions, body language, actions—that you can then factor into how you show up. Empathy is a great self-check skill: To improve your leadership, you could do no worse than to enter into every engagement with another human being reminding yourself to be empathetic first and foremost.

As is the case with all the skills in this book, empathy is a choice, and it is most certainly a skill that most of us can develop. In education reform circles, it is also one of those words that may be over-saturated, tossed around as jargon to the point that educators now may raise skeptical eyebrows. This is unfortunate, because it is difficult to imagine an effective leader lacking empathy. Even if your school community is not as diverse as Jersey City, NJ, the most diverse city in the United States, there still are people who are not the same as you. Empathy suggests you should do the work necessary to understand how those different lives feel.

This week you will have opportunities to reflect on and practice empathy as you go about your days. Pay attention to when you are more and less readily able to exhibit empathy, because these patterns will provide you with detailed insights into how to improve your leadership practice. We also want to point out that you might wish to move back and forth between this skill and the synergistic skills **4.1 Communication, 4.3 Relationship Building, and 4.4 Teamwork.**

3.2 DAY 1: Empathy

|||||||||||||||||||||||||||||||||||||||||||||||||||||||||||||||||||||||||||||||||||||||||||||||||||||||||||||||||||||||||||||||

☆ *"Empathy is seeing with the eyes of another, listening with the ears of another and feeling with the heart of another."* —Alfred Adler

Reflection for Today: Where do you think your empathy skills are most developed—seeing, listening, or feeling through the lens of another person? Which of your empathy skills requires the most development?

_____

_____

_____

_____

List one thing you're grateful for today:

_____

Check the Feeling Wheel inside the front cover and list any emotion(s) you are feeling.

3.2 DAY 2: Empathy

☆ *"Leadership is about empathy."* —Oprah Winfrey

Reflection for Today: Consider your definition of leadership (and if you don't have one, now would be a good time to write a quick draft). Does empathy play a part in that definition? If not, should it? Why or why not?

_____

_____

_____

_____

_____

_____

List one thing you're grateful for today:

Check the Feeling Wheel inside the front cover and list any emotion(s) you are feeling.

Module 3

3.2 DAY 3: Empathy

☆ *"If speaking is silver, then listening is gold."*
—Turkish Proverb

Practice for Today: Hold yourself accountable today to maintain a 90:10 listening to speaking ratio in every interaction you have. What do you notice today compared to other days when you haven't attempted to maintain such a ratio?

List one thing you're grateful for today:

Check the Feeling Wheel inside the front cover and list any emotion(s) you are feeling.

3.2 DAY 4: Empathy

☆ *"If you can learn a simple trick, Scout, you'll get along a lot better with all kinds of folks. You never really understand a person until you consider things from his point of view until you climb inside of his skin and walk around in it."* —Atticus Finch in *To Kill a Mockingbird* (1962)

Practice for Today: Pick a member of your school community who is **most different** from you. Now, try to live and see as much of your day first through that person's eyes. What do you notice about how that person's experience might be different from your own in your school?

_____

_____

List one thing you're grateful for today:

_____

Check the Feeling Wheel inside the front cover and list any emotion(s) you are feeling.

3.2 DAY 5: Empathy

 "Empathy grows as we learn." —Alice Miller

Leadership Considerations: This week, you reflected on and practiced developing empathy. As you think more about this skill, consider these questions:

1. Imagine that you have mastered empathy. What about your leadership practice would be different?

2. Who in your community will most benefit from an improvement in your capacity to be empathetic? How quickly could you bring about that change?

3. Review all the notes you took this week and find your one best thought. Now go share your insight with somebody who might benefit from it.

Weekly Effort	1	2	3	4	5
	none	minimal	some	moderate	significant

Weekly Impact	1	2	3	4	5

Check the Feeling Wheel inside the front cover and list any emotion(s) you are feeling.

WEEK 3.3: Appreciating Diversity

Appreciating diversity begins with recognizing a universal truth: We are all bound together by the commonality of our humanity. Through the mastery of other SEL skills, such as self-perception and empathy, for example, you prepare yourself to see and value the incredible range of experience and wisdom that every other human being has to offer you.

Take a moment, though, to focus on the word *appreciating*. There is a difference between recognizing or even acknowledging diversity and appreciating diversity. In a truly authentic way, appreciating diversity means valuing that diversity as a core strength and opportunity implicit in every interaction you have with others. Appreciating diversity suggests that you are capable of demonstrating with your words and actions that appreciation; that you can do so with a sophistication that reflects a *past investment* in learning about what it might be like to live as someone other than yourself. When you engage in practicing or developing your capacity to be empathetic, you are preparing to appreciate diversity.

It is essential to take the time to understand how others might experience your appreciation of the diversity you observe. It is possible, if not common—especially for people in positions of power like yourself—to demonstrate well-intentioned, but ultimately demeaning, representations of an appreciation of diversity. As you start to appreciate diversity, you will likely find many of the other skills in this book coming into focus.

This week you will have opportunities to reflect on and practice appreciating diversity as you go about your days. Pay extra special attention to how you appreciate diversity because the goal isn't to objectify diversity, but to demonstrate a legitimate, deeply felt regard for the necessity of diversity as part of a more inclusive, and ultimately richer-for-children, learning community. We also want to point out that you might wish to move back and forth between this skill and the synergistic skills **4.1 Communication, 4.2 Social Engagement, and 4.3 Relationship Building.**

3.3 DAY 1: Appreciating Diversity

☆ *"In diversity there is beauty and there is strength."*
—Maya Angelou

Reflection for Today: In what ways is your school diverse? What specific beauty and strength does that diversity produce for your community? What would be lost if your school were less diverse? What might be gained if it were more diverse?

_____

_____

_____

_____

_____

List one thing you're grateful for today:

_____

Check the Feeling Wheel inside the front cover and list any emotion(s) you are feeling.

3.3 DAY 2: Appreciating Diversity

 "Dominator culture has tried to keep us all afraid, to make us choose safety instead of risk, sameness instead of diversity. Moving through that fear, finding out what connects us, reveling in our differences; this is the process that brings us closer, that gives us a world of shared values, of meaningful community." —bell hooks

Reflection for Today: Are there any policies or cultural norms that unintentionally create a place where staff or students are afraid to express diversity? If so, how might you be inadvertently contributing to that culture or what might you be able to do to help your community move away from fear and closer to connection?

List one thing you're grateful for today:

Check the Feeling Wheel inside the front cover and list any emotion(s) you are feeling.

3.3 DAY 3: Appreciating Diversity

||||||||||||||||||||||||||||||||||||||||||||||||||||||||||||||||||||||||||||||||||||||||||||||||||||||||||||||||||||||||||||||||||||||

 *"We need to help students and parents cherish and preserve the ethnic and cultural diversity that nourishes and strengthens this community—and this nation."* —César Chávez

Practice for Today: List specific and consistent ways in which your school celebrates diversity. Look for practices that, for example, don't relegate Black history to only the month of February, but that integrate an appreciation of diversity into the whole of the school calendar. What conclusions do you draw based on the list you're able to compile?

List one thing you're grateful for today:

Check the Feeling Wheel inside the front cover and list any emotion(s) you are feeling.

3.3 DAY 4: Appreciating Diversity

 "Diversity is not about how we differ. Diversity is about embracing one another's uniqueness."
—Ola Joseph

Practice for Today: Pick the member of your school community you perceive as **most different** from you. Communicate, today, to this person at least one way in which you appreciate the diversity of experience between the two of you and how you are seeking to embrace that diversity to create an even better school environment for children, families, and staff.

_____

_____

_____

_____

List one thing you're grateful for today:

_____

Check the Feeling Wheel inside the front cover and list any emotion(s) you are feeling.

3.3 DAY 5: Appreciating Diversity

 "The wise man belongs to all countries, for the home of a great soul is the whole world." —Democritus

Leadership Considerations: This week, you reflected on and practiced appreciating diversity. As you think more about this skill, consider these questions:

1. To which "countries," or groups, in your community, do you need to travel to more often to be able to represent and model an appreciation for all diversity in your community?

2. Does your community understand that one sign of wisdom and greatness is an appreciation of diversity? If not, how might you help them see the importance of this type of wisdom?

3. Review all the notes you took this week and find your one best thought. Now go share your insight with somebody who might benefit from it.

Weekly Effort	1	2	3	4	5
	none	minimal	some	moderate	significant

Weekly Impact	1	2	3	4	5

Check the Feeling Wheel inside the front cover and list any emotion(s) you are feeling.

WEEK 3.4: Respect for Others

As you conclude the module on social awareness, you will hopefully see a strong relationship between taking perspectives, empathy, and appreciating diversity. All these skills can transform your social awareness so that people feel you have their best interests at heart.

As the nature of work in schools turns more toward teams in which sometimes you lead and sometimes you follow, respecting others is another essential skill to develop. Because you are a leader, it can often be the case that your community will more readily defer to you and your opinions because of fear. However, showing respect for others creates a greater sense of psychological safety, allowing people to take interpersonal risks of speaking up, asking for help, and offering their opinions without fear of reprisal (Edmondson, 2014). Your duty as a leader is to respect others by listening well, creating a safer space for discussions, encouraging opinions, and responding productively to all ideas. In general, you show respect for others by seeing them, hearing them, and caring for them as a professional and person.

As you go through this week and after interactions with others, stop and reflect. Did you listen, acknowledge them as a person, and give their ideas the credit they deserve? We also want to point out that you might wish to move back and forth between this skill and the synergistic skill **4.1 Communication, 4.3 Relationship Building and 4.4 Teamwork.**

3.4 DAY 1: Respect for Others

☆ *"Respect is one of the greatest expressions of love."*
—Miguel Ruiz Angel

Reflection for Today: As you look across your staff, students, and community, to whom are you showing the most respect and why? Where might you be struggling with showing respect? Why?

_____

_____

_____

_____

_____

List one thing you're grateful for today:

_____

Check the Feeling Wheel inside the front cover and list any emotion(s) you are feeling.

3.4 DAY 2: Respect for Others

⭐ *"Respect is appreciation of the separateness of the other person, of the ways in which he or she is unique."* —Annie Gottlieb

Reflection for Today: Where are you allowing people to be their unique selves? How does this respect show up in your leadership?

_____

_____

_____

_____

_____

List one thing you're grateful for today:

_____

Check the Feeling Wheel inside the front cover and list any emotion(s) you are feeling.

3.4 DAY 3: Respect for Others

⭐ *"If we lose love and self-respect for each other, this is how we finally die."* —Maya Angelou

Practice for Today: For today, think about somebody with whom you may struggle to show respect. Go out of your way today to offer them a word of kindness.

List one thing you're grateful for today:

Check the Feeling Wheel inside the front cover and list any emotion(s) you are feeling.

3.4 DAY 4: Respect for Others

 "I speak to everyone in the same way, whether he is the garbage man or the president of the university."
—Albert Einstein

Practice for Today: Today, note how you speak to different people: teachers, students, staff members, parents. Do you change your tone, what you say, and how you say it depending on to whom you're speaking? Might any groups experience that as disrespectful?

List one thing you're grateful for today:

Check the Feeling Wheel inside the front cover and list any emotion(s) you are feeling.

3.4 DAY 5: Respect for Others

☆ *"We are all equal in the fact that we are all different. We are all the same in the fact that we will never be the same. We are united by the reality that all colors and all cultures are distinct and individual."* —C. JoyBell C.

Leadership Considerations: This week, you reflected on and practiced respecting others. As you think more about this skill, consider these questions:

1. As a leader, how do you, or how might you, maintain a sense of respect for others, especially when you may feel disrespected? Or, when you feel disrespected, how can you continue to show respect for others?

2. How do you see respect related to the other skills of perspective taking, empathy, and appreciating diversity? Are there groups in your school who could benefit from understanding how all these skills work together?

3. Review all the notes you took this week and find your one best thought. Now go share your insight with somebody who might benefit from it.

Weekly Effort	1	2	3	4	5
	none	minimal	some	moderate	significant

Weekly Impact	1	2	3	4	5

Check the Feeling Wheel inside the front cover and list any emotion(s) you are feeling.

MODULE THREE

Reflection and Action Planning

1. What do you see as the key ideas to continue to think and learn about in this module?

2. Are there any skills from the diagnostic or your initial practice attempts you want to keep working on? If you haven't done so already, add the skill to your action plan.

Module Effort	1	2	3	4	5
	none	minimal	some	moderate	significant

Module Impact	1	2	3	4	5

Check the Feeling Wheel inside the front cover and list any emotion(s) you are feeling.

MODULE 4: RELATIONSHIP SKILLS

Module 3 explores social awareness. It examines how becoming more socially aware is about looking outward to learn about others, and how taking perspectives, empathizing, appreciating diversity, and respecting others allow you to understand other people better. In this module, you will begin to explore relationship building as the counterpart to social awareness. Just because you might understand somebody better does not assure that you will have a meaningful relationship with them. It takes further work and further skills to develop purposeful relationships with students, staff, and parents.

> Just because you might understand somebody better does not assure that you will have a meaningful relationship with them.

CASEL (n.d.) defines the competency of relationship skills as "[t]he abilities to establish and maintain healthy and supportive relationships and to effectively navigate settings with diverse individuals and groups. The ability to communicate clearly, listen well, cooperate with others, resist inappropriate social pressure, negotiate conflict constructively, and seek and offer help when needed." This set of skills is the basis for culture, as strong cultures require positive relationships.

With this brief definition in mind, read the following short narrative of an instructional coach. Notice how she applies her relationship skills to a contentious middle school team, and whether you face similar situations in your school.

Mrs. Jefferson was an instructional coach at a middle school. She had started as a science teacher in the same school, but over her 15-year career, she had learned a great deal about literacy, math, personalized learning, and classroom management. As a coach, she also helped lead the intervention model at her school in response to increasing poverty levels and diversity levels over the past five years. Her school had also been implementing more personalized learning, so teachers had more time for small group instruction and to develop student agency.

As Mrs. Jefferson walked down the hall to the sixth-grade team meeting, she again practiced how she would open the meeting to set a positive tone. Of all the teams she worked with, the sixth-grade team was the most challenging. Many of them had been in the same role for years and had created a team culture that could be considered overly protective of their time and methods. Although there were a few younger team members, they had started to become influenced by some veteran team members.

Nearing the door, Mrs. Jefferson took a deep breath to calm her nerves and put a smile on her face. She entered the room where the team was meeting. Even before sitting down, she made eye contact with one of the younger teachers, Miss Ackley, to see if she could detect her anxiety level. She asked Mrs. Winchel, with whom she had struggled in the past, how her sick husband was feeling. Mr. Sanchez, the veteran of the group, greeted her and, in a sarcastic tone, asked her what brilliance she had brought with her today. Calming herself internally, Mrs. Jefferson just smiled and laughed.

The sixth-grade team had been the last to move toward more personalized learning, throwing up many roadblocks along the way. Nonetheless, they had made some progress, focusing on small group instruction to support more students who had entered their school below grade level. To start the meeting, Mrs. Jefferson opened with a quick check in to set the emotional tone for the meeting, asking each teacher to consider which student had benefited most from last week's small group instruction. She smiled at each and acknowledged each effort. To end, she led a self-congratulatory pat on the back and beamed at how far they had come. This small boost to morale always made the group laugh.

Next, Mrs. Jefferson led with her usual explanation about creating psychological safety and why it was essential to open up, share successes and failures, and support one another through failures. This type of safety had been hard for this team, but she had asked the newer teachers to model this so that the more veteran teachers could help them think through what to do. Today, Mrs. Winchel asked for support on keeping other students on task when working with her small groups. Two months ago, she would sit in meetings with her arms folded, but now she was willing to surface areas of need. Mrs. Jefferson had spent numerous hours with her in one-on-one sessions, working to boost her self-efficacy. She'd seen Mrs. Winchel reinvigorate her teaching and passion for students.

Mrs. Jefferson beamed over how far Mrs. Winchel and this team had come and recognized how far they still needed to go to become a high-functioning team.

Research Basis on Relationship Skills

From a neural perspective, when individuals gather together in a group, neural links are made, and our brains begin to connect on two levels (Goleman, 2006). The first level, called *the low road*, works in the background and always searches for information that can give you implicit signals. For instance, Mrs. Jefferson always scanned how people looked or responded when others were talking to gauge reactions or emotions. The second level, called *the high road*, consists of the specific forms of communication used in groups. For instance, using a predetermined check-in helped Mrs. Jefferson set the emotional tone, and create meaning that the work the team was doing impacted students. Mrs. Jefferson also used social engagement to let people know she cared about them as people as well as teachers and worked hard to make quality connections with all team members so they felt valued. She also impressed on them the idea of psychological safety and its importance for learning from failures and successes. In essence, relationship building is not only about how well people get along but also how well they engage one another, how well they can confide in one another, and ultimately how well they can learn from one another. All these factors are critical to improving teaching and learning in a school.

Throughout this team meeting, Mrs. Jefferson and the sixth-grade team demonstrated improving relationship skills necessary for effective teamwork, implementation, and learning. All teams and the associated social actions essential to improve schools depend on a significant degree of relationship skills. Great relationships act as the energy for forwarding movement on any team. Relationship skills are not developed as an end in and of themselves, but as a condition that allows trust, support, and learning to emerge over time. No matter your role in leading a team, a department, or an entire school, knowing how to develop and use relationship skills can lead to better adult culture and learning.

The CASEL Framework lays out four distinct skill areas that you need to consider to grow your relationship skills:

- Communication
- Social engagement
- Relationship building
- Teamwork

Why Relationship Skills are Critical for Leaders

For the most part, as an educational leader, you do not have a direct influence on students and their achievement and growth. You only have an indirect influence. Renowned educational leadership researcher Kenneth Leithwood and others (2017) explains this as leaders having four distinct but indirect paths to student learning, as discussed in the introduction. As Leithwood translates, leaders can use a rational path, which is primarily about influencing the instructional program or a family path to work with parents. Leaders can also work along the organizational path to change a school's culture and schoolwide experience. Last, leaders can work to influence the emotional path or how you can directly influence teachers' emotions, thoughts, and beliefs (Leithwood & Seashore-Louis, 2012).

You could say that relationship skills are essential to develop no matter the path you choose to influence. However, you could also interpret from Leithwood's research that the organizational and emotional paths, influencing the school's culture and teachers' emotions, have the most impact. Said differently, by building direct relationships with teachers and developing a positive culture, leaders have the most influence.

> By building direct relationships with teachers and developing a positive culture, leaders have the most influence.

As leaders, you can ultimately work along the emotional path by using the skills in this module and focusing on creating high-quality connections and enhancing psychological safety or minimizing the perception people have related to interpersonal threats in their work environment.

MODULE 4: RELATIONSHIP SKILLS

In this module you will learn more about Relationship Skills through

Week 4.1: Communication

Week 4.2: Social Engagement

Week 4.3: Relationship Building

Week 4.4: Teamwork

WEEK 4.1: Communication

Developing productive and meaningful relationships with others relies on communication. Without a doubt, communication skills are the primary means by which you, as a leader, can influence others and help them grow. Your message, tone, and tenor act as the vehicle by which your ideas and thoughts are delivered. Excellent communication is an interpretive system in which you and others try to make sense of each other. As a leader, communicating well supports developing good relationships and also shapes how well your community understands the school's direction and actions you take.

From a positive psychology perspective, excellent communication also integrates the voices of others in that it is inclusive, respectful, and supportive. Excellent positive dialogue is also constructive and seeks to make things better; It doesn't criticize ideas or people. Constructive forms of communication are solution-focused, future-oriented, and collaborative in their intent. These forms of communication define the heart of leadership (Browning, Morris, & Kee, 2013).

So beyond the general nature of speaking clearly, listening well, and being truthful, excellent communication requires your deliberate attention and intent. Sometimes our usual ways of communicating do not serve us well as leaders. Even though people need you to set direction, they also want to be heard and acknowledged. In this way, you create stronger relationships and can use your influence along multiple paths. As you work through this week's prompts, think about if and how your communication is clear, integrates with others, and builds a mutual feeling of trust in your school.

We also want to point out that you might wish to move back and forth between this skill and the synergistic skills **3.1 Perspective Taking, 3.3 Appreciating Diversity, and 3.4 Respect for Others.**

Module 4

4.1 DAY 1: Communication

☆ *"The single biggest problem in communication is the illusion that it has taken place."* —George Bernard Shaw

Reflection for Today: Which messages that you are trying to communicate don't seem to be landing very well with others? Why do you think that is?

List one thing you're grateful for today:

Check the Feeling Wheel inside the front cover and list any emotion(s) you are feeling.

4.1 DAY 2: Communication

⭐ *"My belief is that communication is the best way to create strong relationships."* —Jada Pinkett Smith

Reflection for Today: How well do you use communication to develop relationships? How well do you communicate in the relationship?

List one thing you're grateful for today:

Check the Feeling Wheel inside the front cover and list any emotion(s) you are feeling.

4.1 DAY 3: Communication

☆ *"I do feel a responsibility to try and raise awareness and to help tell the stories of those who may not otherwise have a voice."* —Gemma Chan

Practice for Today: As you work with individuals or teams today, how can you better understand their perspective? How can you include their view in your communication?

_____

_____

_____

_____

List one thing you're grateful for today:

_____

Check the Feeling Wheel inside the front cover and list any emotion(s) you are feeling.

4.1 DAY 4: Communication

☆ *"Although our body language governs the way other people perceive us, our body language also governs how we perceive ourselves and how those perceptions become reinforced through our own behavior, our interactions, and even our physiology."* —Amy Cuddy

Practice for Today: As you think about your body language, what messages are you conveying? Today, practice a more positive and relational form of body language and think about the impact of that on others and yourself.

List one thing you're grateful for today:

Check the Feeling Wheel inside the front cover and list any emotion(s) you are feeling.

4.1 DAY 5: Communication

⭐ *"Words are singularly the most powerful force available to humanity. We can choose to use this force constructively with words of encouragement, or destructively using words of despair. Words have energy and power with the ability to help, to heal, to hinder, to hurt, to harm, to humiliate and to humble."* —Yehuda Berg

Leadership Considerations: This week, you began thinking about your communication skills to develop healthy relationships. As you end this week, consider these questions:

1. How are your words and messages inclusive, respectful, and supportive of others?
2. Are your messages solution-focused, future-oriented, and collaborative in their intent?
3. Review all the notes you took this week and find your one best thought. Now go share your insight with somebody who might benefit from it.

Weekly Effort	1	2	3	4	5
	none	minimal	some	moderate	significant

Weekly Impact	1	2	3	4	5

Check the Feeling Wheel inside the front cover and list any emotion(s) you are feeling.

WEEK 4.2: Social Engagement

This book focuses on you. It's meant to support you, first and foremost, in developing your understanding and proficiency regarding the CASEL Framework's competencies. In some modules, such as self-awareness, the internal focus is implicit in the name of the skill itself. This week's skill—social engagement— presents you with a bit more tension between focusing on your inward-facing skills and your outward-facing skills. By definition, interactions with others must be part of your practice this week.

Let's start by clarifying the concept of social engagement. Social engagement is characterized by actions like volunteering at a workday at your school or organizing a meal train for a community member in need. Typically, social engagement unites individuals through a commonality: a commitment to a mission or organization or the pursuit of a specific kind of engagement or change. Although the form (volunteering, donating money) and rationale of social engagement may vary (shared desire to bring about change or a shared commitment to an organization), a critical concept underlies all optimal and equitable social engagement: trust.

You must internalize just how impactful the presence and absence of trust are to social engagement. In your community, if you observe that particular populations regularly do not engage in social activities at your school, it may be that this group lacks trust in the organization in one way or another. If communities or individuals feel threatened by school leadership, it is highly unlikely that they will be excited to engage socially. If other community members have betrayed groups, it is doubtful that those who feel betrayed can trust others. If you lead across difference, you might do well to assume—if you do not already know—that there are trust issues in your community.

> If communities or individuals feel threatened by school leadership, it is highly unlikely that they will be excited to engage socially.

Though this only scratches the surface of social engagement, this week, you will have the opportunity to focus on how you are or are not contributing to the development of trust in your school community. Without trust, there can be no social engagement.

We also want to point out that you might wish to move back and forth between this skill and the synergistic skills **3.1 Perspective Taking, 3.3 Appreciating Diversity, and 3.4 Respect for Others.**

4.2 DAY 1: Social Engagement

☆ *"The best way to find out if you can trust somebody is to trust them."* —Ernest Hemingway

Reflection for Today: How trusting are you of other people in your community? How easy do you make it for others to trust you? How do you know?

_____

_____

_____

_____

_____

_____

List one thing you're grateful for today:

_____

Check the Feeling Wheel inside the front cover and list any emotion(s) you are feeling.

Module 4

4.2 DAY 2: Social Engagement

 "The best partnerships aren't dependent on a mere common goal but on a shared path of equality, desire, and no small amount of passion."
—Sarah MacLean

Reflection for Today: How united is your school community regarding your school's mission or goals? What have you done or what could you do to increase the equality, desire, and passion between all partners toward those goals?

_____

_____

_____

_____

List one thing you're grateful for today:

_____

Check the Feeling Wheel inside the front cover and list any emotion(s) you are feeling.

4.2 DAY 3: Social Engagement

⭐ *"The most common way people give up their power is by thinking they don't have any."* —Alice Walker

Practice for Today: Write down the structures, processes, or people your school uses that are intended to bring people together. How many are healthy and yielding the results you seek? How do you know? How many aren't quite so healthy, and what might you do to improve them?

_____

_____

_____

_____

_____

List one thing you're grateful for today:

_____

Check the Feeling Wheel inside the front cover and list any emotion(s) you are feeling.

Module 4

4.2 DAY 4: Social Engagement

 "The intention and outcome of vulnerability is trust, intimacy and connection." —Brené Brown

Practice for Today: Attempt to become a little more vulnerable with someone in your school. Choose someone you suspect does not trust you. Make a phone call to the person or provide them with an unexpected resource. See if you can increase trust, even if only a little bit, and thus the possibility for eventual increased social engagement.

_____

_____

_____

_____

List one thing you're grateful for today:

_____

Check the Feeling Wheel inside the front cover and list any emotion(s) you are feeling.

Module 4

4.2 DAY 5: Social Engagement

 "Trust starts with truth and ends with truth."
—Santosh Kalwar

Leadership Considerations: This week, you reflected on and practiced social engagement, with an explicit focus on the bedrock requirement of trust. As you think more about this skill, consider these questions:

1. Are you 100% truthful with your community? If not, why not? What's holding you back?

2. Are you 100% honest with yourself? If not, why not? What's holding you back?

3. Review all the notes you took this week and find your one best thought. Now go share your insight with somebody who might benefit from it.

Weekly Effort	1	2	3	4	5
	none	minimal	some	moderate	significant

Weekly Impact	1	2	3	4	5

Check the Feeling Wheel inside the front cover and list any emotion(s) you are feeling.

WEEK 4.3: Relationship Building

Like social engagement, relationship building, by definition, involves more than just you. Like all other skills for developing healthy relationships, this skill depends on the consistency and quality of your more individual work in areas like self-management. Relationship-building begins with a strong sense of your internal capabilities.

Relationship building, we find, is a particularly well-named skill in that *building* conveys the hard work implicit in mastering this skill. In some cases, you will find that you will need to build relationships action by action, slowly and painstakingly proving your interest in connecting with others and valuing their presence, participation, and contributions to the community. You will need to see and acknowledge your own mistakes that can weaken or destroy relationships and start the relationship rebuilding process.

You will need to get comfortable with the likelihood that not all community members may want to be in the same kind of relationship that you envision. The burden is still yours, though, to understand, accept, and find other ways to ensure that all members of your community can build the relationships necessary to better your school.

Relationship building presumes there is something shared across at least two people and that that something justifies the investment of their time and energy in the advancement of the relationship. Importantly, the goal of relationship building does not have to be everyone wanting to have dinner together every Saturday night. Within your school community, healthy relationships will ideally organize around a well-understood and shared commitment to the school's goals for children. How you, as a leader, create and nurture others' agency to define and establish relationships within the school community will contribute significantly to the quality and quantity of relationship building that takes place.

This week you'll have the opportunity to focus on relationship building: how you do it, with whom, and how you might improve and scale relationships throughout your school.

We also want to point out that you might wish to move back and forth between this skill and the synergistic skills **3.1 Perspective Taking, 3.2 Empathy, and 3.3 Appreciating Diversity.**

4.3 DAY 1: Relationship Building

||||||||||||||||||||||||||||||||||||||||||||||||||||||||||||||||||||||||||||||||||||||||||||||||||||||||||||||||||||||

☆ *"Each friend represents a world in us, a world possibly not born until they arrive, and it is only by this meeting that a new world is born."* —Anaïs Nin

Reflection for Today: How do you view the possibility of creating new relationships in your community? Do you run toward those opportunities or find yourself avoiding this part of your work? Why might that be?

_____

_____

_____

_____

_____

List one thing you're grateful for today:

_____

Check the Feeling Wheel inside the front cover and list any emotion(s) you are feeling.

Module 4

4.3 DAY 2: Relationship Building

☆ *"Lots of people want to ride with you in the limo, but what you want is someone who will take the bus with you when the limo breaks down."* —Oprah Winfrey

Reflection for Today: How many people in your community would take the bus with you when something breaks down at school? What characterizes those relationships? How might you strengthen your relationships with your community to increase the number of people who would get on the bus?

_____

_____

_____

_____

List one thing you're grateful for today:

_____

Check the Feeling Wheel inside the front cover and list any emotion(s) you are feeling.

4.3 DAY 3: Relationship Building

|||||||||||||||||||||||||||||||||||||||||||||||||||||||||||||||||||||||||||||||||||||||||||||||||||||||||||||

☆ *"No road is long with good company."* —Turkish Proverb

Practice for Today: Think about one person in your community with whom you have a neutral or slightly positive relationship. What can you do today to move that relationship into a more positive territory? How might you show that person that you value the relationship?

_____

_____

_____

_____

_____

List one thing you're grateful for today:

_____

Check the Feeling Wheel inside the front cover and list any emotion(s) you are feeling.

Module 4

4.3 DAY 4: Relationship Building

 "Love takes off masks that we fear we cannot live without and know we cannot live within."
—James Baldwin

Practice for Today: Leaders too often believe they must always project strength and expertise. Is that you? See if you can take off that mask in front of at least one person with whom you do not have a healthy relationship and who has less real or perceived power in your community. Notice what it feels like to cede or share any amount of power with someone with whom you've never done this before and whether or not you can sense even a small change in your relationship with that person.

_____

_____

_____

List one thing you're grateful for today:

_____

Check the Feeling Wheel inside the front cover and list any emotion(s) you are feeling.

4.3 DAY 5: Relationship Building

☆ *"Never look down on anybody unless you're helping them up."* —Jesse Jackson

Leadership Considerations: This week, you reflected on and practiced relationship building. As you think more about this skill, consider these questions:

1. Are you helping everybody in your community up, or might you be looking down on some people? How do you know?

2. Is anybody in your community looking down on you? How might you take responsibility for giving them reasons to help you up?

3. Review all the notes you took this week and find your one best thought. Now go share your insight with somebody who might benefit from it.

Weekly Effort	1	2	3	4	5
	none	minimal	some	moderate	significant
Weekly Impact	1	2	3	4	5

Check the Feeling Wheel inside the front cover and list any emotion(s) you are feeling.

Module 4

WEEK 4.4: Teamwork

The last skill in this module is teamwork. Since teams have become the primary structure for how work gets done in most organizations, including schools, productive relationships will strengthen teams' capacity to deliver more and better results for children.

Although there are thousands of books and guides on building effective teams, teamwork eventually needs to become more of an action than a set of ideas. That orientation, termed *teaming*, is "a process of bringing together skills and ideas from disparate areas to produce something new—something that no one individual, or even a group in one area of expertise, could do alone" (Edmondson, 2014). As schools look to innovate in many areas, teamwork and teaming requires considerable relationship skills so that people will share, learn, and grow from their collective actions.

Edmondson (2014) suggests that "[h]igh-quality teaming blends getting to know people quickly—their knowledge, skills, and goals—with listening to other points of view, coordinating actions, and making shared decisions." As a leader in your school, your ability to analyze your teams' needs and support them in improving their teamwork through enhanced relationship skills will be essential. As you work through this week's module, consider how teams are different from teaming, and how strong relationships help make innovation move quicker.

We also want to point out that you might wish to move back and forth between this skill and the synergistic skills **3.1 Perspective Taking, 3.2 Empathy, and 3.4 Respect for Others.**

4.4 DAY 1: Teamwork

☆ *"Unity is strength . . . when there is teamwork and collaboration, wonderful things can be achieved."*
—Mattie Stepanek

Reflection for Today: As you think about your school's adult teams, how unified are they? How are you helping them develop more unity through relationship skills?

_____

_____

_____

_____

_____

List one thing you're grateful for today:

_____

Check the Feeling Wheel inside the front cover and list any emotion(s) you are feeling.

4.4 DAY 2: Teamwork

☆ *"Teamwork is the secret that makes common people achieve uncommon results."* —Ifeanyi Enoch Onuoha

Reflection for Today: Which of your teams is getting uncommon results? What are they doing differently with their teamwork, and how can you spread that to other teams?

_____

_____

_____

_____

_____

List one thing you're grateful for today:

_____

Check the Feeling Wheel inside the front cover and list any emotion(s) you are feeling.

4.4 DAY 3: Teamwork

☆ *"None of us, including me, ever do great things. But we can all do small things, with great love, and together we can do something wonderful."*
—Mother Teresa

Practice for Today: What is the wonderful thing your teams are creating? How clear is that to them? How can you make it clearer for them?

_____

_____

_____

_____

List one thing you're grateful for today:

_____

Check the Feeling Wheel inside the front cover and list any emotion(s) you are feeling.

4.4 DAY 4: Teamwork

☆ *"Don't make assumptions. Find the courage to ask questions and to express what you really want. Communicate with others as clearly as you can to avoid misunderstandings, sadness and drama. With just this one agreement, you can completely transform your life."* —Don Miguel Ruiz

Practice for Today: Observe some of your teams as they meet. What assumptions or mindsets might they be holding? How can you help surface these?

List one thing you're grateful for today:

Check the Feeling Wheel inside the front cover and list any emotion(s) you are feeling.

4.4 DAY 5: Teamwork

☆ *"Well-designed teams are those with clear goals, well-thought-out tasks that are conducive to teamwork, team members with the right skills and experiences for the task, adequate resources, and access to coaching and support."* —Amy Edmondson

Leadership Considerations: This week, you explored the nature of teamwork or teaming as an action. As you end this week, consider the following questions.

1. Are the qualities of a well-designed team in place in your teams? How can you coach and support them?

2. How would you describe the relationships on each of your school's teams? Are they helpful or discouraging people from sharing openly and learning?

3. Review all the notes you took this week and find your one best thought. Now go share your insight with somebody who might benefit from it.

Weekly Effort	1	2	3	4	5
	none	minimal	some	moderate	significant

Weekly Impact	1	2	3	4	5

Check the Feeling Wheel inside the front cover and list any emotion(s) you are feeling.

1. What do you see as the key ideas to continue to think and learn about in this module?

2. Are there any skills from the diagnostic or your initial practice attempts you want to keep working on? If you haven't done so already, add these skills to your action plan.

Module Effort	1	2	3	4	5
	none	minimal	some	moderate	significant

Module Impact	1	2	3	4	5

Check the Feeling Wheel inside the front cover and list any emotion(s) you are feeling.

MODULE 5: RESPONSIBLE DECISION MAKING

||||||||||||||||||||||||||||||||||||||||||||||||||||||||||||||||||||||||||||||||||||||||||||||||||||||||||||

Responsible Decision Making, the fifth module in this book, is how you enact or energize all the other competencies. Whether you are deciding how to discuss an issue with a teacher, or how to improve team relationships, you need first to determine how to make those decisions responsibly. As a school leader, your capacity to make excellent decisions for your community and yourself requires the most enlightened understanding possible in a given moment. Taking a look at just how dense CASEL's summary of this competency is gives you a sense of how complex and nuanced responsible decision making *should* be. Responsible decision making is

> [t]he abilities to make caring and constructive choices about personal behavior and social interactions across diverse situations. This includes the capacities to consider ethical standards and safety concerns, and to evaluate the benefits and consequences of various actions for personal, social and collective well-being. (CASEL, n.d.)

First, notice the social elements in the definition. Here, we're not concerned with how to make better personal decisions only, but whether or not we're making a responsible choice for both our community and ourselves. The obvious implication is that your decision-making practice is responsible only when it can contemplate other stakeholders' perspectives and needs, with authenticity and integrity. Second, notice how many adjectives appear in the definition: *personal, social, ethical,* and *safety.* Entire books could be (and probably have been) written about decision making through the lens of any one of these adjectives. You don't need to take that as your cue to feel overwhelmed, but rather as a reminder that responsible decision making should feel complex when you're doing it right.

What might responsible decision making look like? Consider the following scenario.

> Andrew Truong, the Director of Operations at his school, owns the budget development process each year and has led it for four years. In his fourth year of leading the process, Mr. Truong is applying much of what he's learned—often the hard way—regarding responsible decision making.

The first time Mr. Truong needed to develop a budget, he was blindsided by the calendar and lacked an appreciation of the necessity of using an inclusive process. As a result, the budget proposal that Mr. Truong presented to both his school leader and his board, in public at a regular board meeting, was met with scathing criticism and confusion from all corners of the community. Even though Mr. Truong presented a proposal—not an actual budget for approval—the community experienced his work as a unilateral use of power that excluded necessary and diverse perspectives. How could Mr. Truong have thought that making proposals on everything from teachers' salaries to reductions in summer enrichment programs could be acceptable without input from the community?

Today, Mr. Truong looks forward to collaborating on developing the school's budget. When school starts each year, the entire budget development process is calendared and available to the public. He sets aside time for all stakeholders in the community to:

- Contribute concerns, expectations, perceived opportunities, and general comments months in advance of finalizing the budget. Mr. Truong provides multiple avenues for the community to use to do this, ranging from surveys to in-person meetings he runs that occur at different times during the day to regularly scheduled school finance committee meetings.

- Educate the community about school finance. He explains especially relevant education code (clarifying special needs funding and the school's legal obligations is a perennial hot topic). He also discusses budget creation, the processes other schools use, and the school's external administrators' processes to evaluate the school's budget. Mr. Truong has learned that an uninformed community cannot fully participate in the budget decision-making process effectively.

- Review a summary document that he creates that reflects all the input the community provided. This document forms the foundation for the community to ask clarifying questions, express priorities, and to begin to suggest solutions regarding how to weight expenditures in the budget.

- Vote on the top three budget priorities. Though not an official vote, each community member can indicate their top three preferences via a simple survey or phone call.

(Continued)

(Continued)

- Provide intermittent debriefs on the quality of the process to-date. These check-ins allow Mr. Truong to reveal gaps in the process and ensure that the community is feeling engaged and informed.

- Plan to attend critical decision-making meetings. Mr. Truong makes sure that the community hears—repeatedly—when the most impactful budget process meetings are going to occur so that the community can attend, if at all possible. For some of these particularly essential meetings (such as the last meeting before budget submission), Mr. Truong organizes childcare to make attending the meeting as easy as possible.

- Debrief on the overall budget decision-making process so that any learnings can be applied to next year's process.

Research Basis on Responsible Decision Making

You make hundreds of decisions daily as a human being. You decide when to get up, what to wear, and where to spend your time after work. Now, couple that with the hundreds or more decisions in a day you get to make a school leader, and you can see why this is such a critical competency for excellence. The history of research about decision making has explored the most rational ways people make decisions. However, for our purposes and in line with social-emotional understanding, most decision-making research today focuses on the role your emotional side plays in the process.

As a school leader, you want to believe you are making the most rational decisions for the most people. Still, plenty of research has shown that your cognitive and personal biases guide your decision making without you knowing it (Kahneman, 2011). As a school leader, some of the cognitive biases that may interfere with your decision making include

- confirmation bias in which you only look for evidence that supports your conclusion,

- anchoring in which all decisions are influenced by initial information,

- repetition bias in which you tend to believe the information you hear more frequently,

- overconfidence bias in which you make decisions without the facts, and

- groupthink in which you feel pressure to conform to the opinions of a larger group.

While numerous cognitive biases can interfere with responsible decision making, just knowing that these biases exist can help. Similar to ideas discussed about self-awareness, knowing these biases and which ones tend to influence your decision making can assist you in making better and more responsible decisions for yourself and your community.

Here are six distinct skill areas that you need to consider to grow your, and your community's, responsible decision-making skills:

- Identifying problems

- Analyzing situations

- Solving problems

- Evaluating

- Reflecting

- Ethical responsibility

Mr. Truong did not get all these, or possibly any of these, right the first time. You will benefit from his experience, and this week's prompts to help you improve on and ideally avoid some of Mr. Truong's initial missteps, which may have been caused by his cognitive biases. It is more important to make progress in developing these skills than it is to expect and experience perfection. Over time, Mr. Truong developed a responsible decision-making process that recognized how central time management is to support a more responsible decision-making practice. Again, you already know going into the school year that time will be at a premium. You can use that insight to create the necessary time and responsible decision-making conditions that will contribute to better overall decisions for students and happier, more engaged stakeholders.

Why Responsible Decision-Making Skills Are Critical for Leaders

Fundamentally, every decision you make as a school leader reflects your values and a demonstration of your power. The demands of your role and the timeline on which so many of your tasks must occur do not often lend themselves to modeling responsible decision making. Still, you can seek to evolve your practice to consider those constraints as often as possible. Particularly within diverse communities, decision-making processes can either demonstrate sensitivity to disrupting traditional patterns of power, or not. Your strength and influence as a leader can exponentially increase if you embrace the perhaps counterintuitive notion of decreasing your voice's proportional weight in decision-making processes while increasing others' voices. The more that decision making becomes something your community does rather than something you do, the more likely it will be for students to benefit from a given decision.

Implementing responsible and inclusive decision-making practices is almost sure to try your patience, especially if you are just getting started with the concept. Bake this into your process: Expect the frustration, expect the need to go slow to bring all stakeholders along with you and each other, expect backsliding and communication issues and errors. Consider all this, as well as part of your decision-making process. Yes, you are seeking to optimize the way you make better decisions. However, in doing so, you may need to go much slower to go much faster toward increasing outcomes for students.

As leaders, you can ensure more frequent responsible decision making:

- Create space and time for a diverse group of stakeholders to contribute to problem or opportunity definition.

- Establish or adopt defined processes that the school community uses to solve different types of problems. The more complex the problem, likely the more inclusive the process should be.

- Identify a small number of high impact decisions that you know you will have to make during the year. In addition to implementing the previous two bullets, for these particular decisions, schedule time—ahead of time—to debrief and learn from what worked and didn't work for the stakeholders involved in the decision-making process.

- Co-create a culture of ethical responsibility. What norms might your community adopt to increase all stakeholders' trust that the decision-making process is transparent, representative, and ultimately focused on advancing students' well-being?

- Build into your process a method to check your own and others' biases.

You can begin to create these conditions or iterate on your school's existing conditions as you focus on the following six skills.

MODULE 5: RESPONSIBLE DECISION MAKING

In this module you will learn more about Responsible Decision Making through

Week 5.1: Identifying Problems

Week 5.2: Analyzing Situations

Week 5.3: Solving Problems

Week 5.4: Evaluating

Week 5.5: Reflecting

Week 5.6: Ethical Responsibility

WEEK 5.1: Identifying Problems

||||||||||||||||||||||||||||||||||||||||||||||||||||||||||||||||||||||||||||||||||||||||||||||||||||||||||||||||||||||||||||||||||||||||||||||||||||||||||||||||||||||||||||||||||||||||||||||||

If you asked us to identify our top three to five skills to master in this book, this one is highly likely to appear in that list. Make no mistake: Identifying and defining problems is absolutely a skill, and it's a skill that is not taught explicitly to school leaders. Other disciplines do teach students how to identify and craft problems or opportunity statements. For example, in product design programs, students practice need finding. Need finding encourages students to observe carefully during their everyday lives, and capture the needs, or frustrations that come to the surface. In doing so, students begin to understand how to observe the world with an eye for problems and opportunity identification and to recognize how differently each of us might define the same problem or opportunity.

Identifying problems well also requires attention to precise language. There is a huge difference between the following two problems, even though they mean to address the same thing:

- Our school has an attendance problem.
- Students who live the farthest away from our school, and farthest away from a public transportation hub, have the lowest attendance rates in our school despite equally valuing their education.

The first example too often reflects the level at which schools can define problems. Our systems and improvement plans typically do not define problems beyond this level of specificity. The second example, however, begins to provide critical degrees of focus. The second example narrows the problem space down to students who live the farthest away from school, and who live the farthest away from a transportation hub. If we are stuck trying to solve a poorly defined attendance problem, as we would be in the first example, we should have little hope of finding a breakthrough solution. However, the second example gives us the gift of additional focus, increasing the possibility of finding an eventual solution to a much better-defined problem.

This week you'll focus on developing your capacity to identify not just any problems but sound problems; problems that are worth your time and energy. This skill might be a particularly good one to return to because the return on your investment in strengthening this skill will save you untold amounts of time, money, and frustration.

We also want to point out that you might wish to move back and forth between this skill and the synergistic skills **2.2 Goal Setting and Productive Habits, 2.5 Stress Management, and 2.6 Self-Discipline.**

5.1 DAY 1: Identifying Problems

☆ *"A problem clearly stated is a problem half solved."*
—Dorothea Brande

Reflection for Today: How well do you identify and define or express problems? What might you need to do differently?

_____

_____

_____

_____

_____

_____

List one thing you're grateful for today:

_____

Check the Feeling Wheel inside the front cover and list any emotion(s) you are feeling.

5.1 DAY 2: Identifying Problems

 *"A problem is a chance for you to do your best."*
—Duke Ellington

Reflection for Today: One of the biggest challenges you face as a school leader is a seemingly impossible list of complex problems to address. But what if you let go of that, at least a little bit, and set yourself up for success on one or two issues you care the most about solving? What are those one or two problems, and have you written excellent problem statements?

_____

_____

_____

_____

_____

List one thing you're grateful for today:

_____

Check the Feeling Wheel inside the front cover and list any emotion(s) you are feeling.

Module 5

5.1 DAY 3: Identifying Problems

☆ *"Problems can become opportunities when the right people come together."* —Robert Redford

Practice for Today: Take a moment to assess a problem you are currently trying to solve at school. Have you brought together the right people to transform the problem into an opportunity? Before investing any more time into solving this problem, make sure you've assembled the best team possible.

List one thing you're grateful for today:

Check the Feeling Wheel inside the front cover and list any emotion(s) you are feeling.

5.1 DAY 4: Identifying Problems

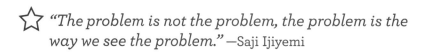 *"The problem is not the problem, the problem is the way we see the problem."* —Saji Ijiyemi

Practice for Today: Ask for feedback on how you've framed a problem *and assume* that you do not clearly see the problem. What mistake or assumption might you have made that prevented you from seeing the problem more accurately?

_____

_____

_____

_____

_____

List one thing you're grateful for today:

_____

Check the Feeling Wheel inside the front cover and list any emotion(s) you are feeling.

Module 5

5.1 DAY 5: Identifying Problems

 "Never be swift to label a situation as a problem—and be careful in ever labelling a person as one."
—Rasheed Oguniaru

Leadership Considerations: This week, you considered how you identify solutions. As you end this week, consider the following questions:

1. How many of the problems you're trying to solve might not be problems? How would you know or assess whether or not you've done this?

2. Have you mistaken people for problems? How might you reframe your problem and shift the source of the problem to a more accurate and productive source?

3. Review all the notes you took this week and find your one best thought. Now go share your insight with somebody who might benefit from it.

Weekly Effort	1	2	3	4	5
	none	minimal	some	moderate	significant
Weekly Impact	1	2	3	4	5

Check the Feeling Wheel inside the front cover and list any emotion(s) you are feeling.

Module 5

WEEK 5.2: Analyzing Situations

In your day-to-day life as a leader in your school, you face a dizzying array of situations that all can go south in a hurry. As part of the decision-making competency, your ability to analyze the situation can accelerate any situation toward a better or worse outcome, depending on your skills.

No classes teach you how to analyze situations in schools. But simply stated, to analyze a situation means that you examine the circumstances, surrounding events, and facts. From this information, you try to identify the risks and priorities to create a plan of action. Leaders with more considerable skills in analyzing situations can more easily identify the most relevant information, make sense of it, and pick out the most essential concerns to address.

This ability to deftly analyze situations also joins forces with your other social and emotional competencies. For instance, think about happening on a crying student in the hall. By recognizing this as a problem, you can immediately engage your empathy skills and check in with the student, or you can engage your rules-based mindset and tell the student to get back to class. Either response may be appropriate depending on the situation, but either response may also be inappropriate based on the social and emotional priorities. The form of social awareness and relationship skill you engage depends on how your abilities to analyze the situation interact with your other competencies.

As you work through various situations this week, analyze how you try to gather information about the situation. Next, consider how you analyze the risks and priorities in the situation. Last, reflect on how other skills like identifying your own emotions, stress management, empathy and diversity, and communication impact your analysis of situations.

We also want to point out that you might wish to move back and forth between this skill and the synergistic skills **1.1 Developing Accurate Self-Perception, 2.5 Stress Management, and 2.6 Self-Discipline.**

5.2 DAY 1: Analyzing Situations

☆ *"When you're an engineer, you want to analyze things a lot. But if you believe that the most important data points are people, then you have to make conclusions in relatively short order."*
—Tim Cook

Reflection for Today: As you think about the way you analyze situations, do you jump to quick conclusions, or do you take time to analyze the risks and priorities in the situation?

_____

_____

_____

_____

List one thing you're grateful for today:

_____

Check the Feeling Wheel inside the front cover and list any emotion(s) you are feeling.

Module 5

5.2 DAY 2: Analyzing Situations

"I'm kind of psychotic and I like to talk about things.
I'm a Virgo, too, so I like to analyze and overprocess."
—Pink

Reflection for Today: Are there ever situations that deserve overprocessing? What circumstances demand more processing versus less processing?

_____

_____

_____

_____

_____

List one thing you're grateful for today:

_____

Check the Feeling Wheel inside the front cover and list any emotion(s) you are feeling.

5.2 DAY 3: Analyzing Situations

☆ *"I over analyze situations because I'm scared of what may happen if I'm not prepared for it."* —Turcois Ominek

Practice for Today: As you enter situations today that may demand your time and attention, what information might you be taking for granted? What parts of the situation do you need to analyze more in-depth?

_____

_____

_____

_____

_____

List one thing you're grateful for today:

_____

Check the Feeling Wheel inside the front cover and list any emotion(s) you are feeling.

5.2 DAY 4: Analyzing Situations

☆ *"My kind of wanting to be funny didn't come from need, necessarily. The closest I can analyze it is that it was an easy way to make friends, I found out. It was just a great kind of social tool."* —Will Ferrell

Practice for Today: Think about a social tool, the use of which you'd like to improve. You might consider humor, empathy, or perhaps a concern for diversity. Think about how you can use this social tool in situations you face today.

_____

_____

_____

_____

_____

List one thing you're grateful for today:

_____

Check the Feeling Wheel inside the front cover and list any emotion(s) you are feeling.

Module 5

5.2 DAY 5: Analyzing Situations

☆ *"I can analyze how I do things, but the actual doing it—when the synapses just start firing—I can't explain."* —Apollo Robbins

Leadership Considerations: This week, you considered how you analyze situations and how you use your other social and emotional skills in this analysis. As you end this week, consider the following questions:

1. Do you have built-in patterns or habits for analyzing situations? How can you slow down to consider more information and think about the risks and priorities for others?

2. Which of your social or emotional skills do you need to practice and use to help you analyze situations differently?

3. Review all the notes you took this week and find your one best thought. Now go share your insight with somebody who might benefit from it.

Weekly Effort	1	2	3	4	5
	none	minimal	some	moderate	significant

Weekly Impact	1	2	3	4	5

Check the Feeling Wheel inside the front cover and list any emotion(s) you are feeling.

Module 5

WEEK 5.3: Solving Problems

As we mentioned briefly in the Identifying Problems skill (Week 5.1 of this module), solving problems effectively depends entirely on how well you identify and define a problem. If you're not confident in your capacity to identify and express issues well, you might want to continue to practice that skill until you've strengthened that aspect of your practice, at least a little bit.

Solving problems requires a well-stated problem; otherwise, you might waste your time with solutions that are ultimately less likely to address your problem. Even if your problem is, perhaps, not well-defined, you can mitigate some of the risk implicit in working with poorly defined problems by keeping your solutions small and working your way up to larger and broader solutions. In education, especially when the cost of failing to solve a problem immediately shows up in students' faces, the tug to solve problems can overwhelm the resolve necessary to put even a dent in some of the challenges we face.

Solving problems also implies that you have a range of concrete strategies that you can apply to problems. For example, crossword puzzlers learn early on to parse clues in a multitude of ways to illuminate the universe of possible answers. That strategy, of considering multiple ways in which the language in a given clue might be parsed, is a precursor to solving the crossword puzzle. Similarly, in our work as leaders, we should be able to point to specific, concrete problem-solving strategies that we use whether we're tackling a complex or less challenging problem.

This week, you'll focus on reviewing how you solve problems; by the end of the week, you should have a more definite sense of just how robust your problem-solving tool kit is and how you might continue to increase its contents.

We also want to point out that you might wish to move back and forth between this skill and the synergistic skills **1.2 Strengths of Emotions and 1.3 Developing Self-Confidence.**

5.3 DAY 1: Solving Problems

☆ *"It is better to solve one problem five different ways, than to solve five problems one way."* —George Pólya

Reflection for Today: How many concrete problem-solving strategies have you mastered? Do you have a diverse and varied toolbox for solving problems, or do you find yourself using the same solutions repeatedly?

List one thing you're grateful for today:

Check the Feeling Wheel inside the front cover and list any emotion(s) you are feeling.

5.3 DAY 2: Solving Problems

 "Never be limited by other people's imaginations."
—Dr. Mae Jemison

Reflection for Today: Consider a problem that you are trying to solve. How might you ensure that your approach to a possible solution reflects a fundamentally different way of thinking compared to the thoughts and actions that led to the problem in the first place?

_____

_____

_____

_____

_____

List one thing you're grateful for today:

_____

Check the Feeling Wheel inside the front cover and list any emotion(s) you are feeling.

5.3 DAY 3: Solving Problems

⟨☆⟩ *"Fall in love with the problem, not the solution."*
  —Various

Practice for Today: Let go of a solution today and commit to revisiting the problem that required the answer you are abandoning. As you re-embrace the problem, try to jot down one to three new possible solutions that may reveal themselves to you.

List one thing you're grateful for today:

Check the Feeling Wheel inside the front cover and list any emotion(s) you are feeling.

5.3 DAY 4: Solving Problems

 "Great leaders are almost always great simplifiers, who can cut through argument, debate, and doubt, to offer a solution everybody can understand."
—Colin Powell

Practice for Today: Look for an opportunity today to practice simplifying a complex problem. Don't pressure yourself to solve the problem or simplify the situation down to its least complex representation. Just spend the day looking for at least one opportunity to focus explicitly on simplifying a complex problem to catalyze opportunities to create better and simpler solutions.

List one thing you're grateful for today:

Check the Feeling Wheel inside the front cover and list any emotion(s) you are feeling.

5.3 DAY 5: Solving Problems

 "Success is a collection of problems solved." –I. M. Pei

Leadership Considerations: This week, you considered how you approach and solve problems, perhaps viewing this topic through some new or challenging lens. As you end this week, consider the following questions:

1. Do you have a system that tracks the problems you are currently facing, as well as successful solutions to past problems?

2. How regularly do you communicate problem and solution statuses with your community? Are you helping your community see any of the successes you've achieved as a result of solving problems?

3. Review all the notes you took this week and find your one best thought. Now go share your insight with somebody who might benefit from it.

Weekly Effort	1	2	3	4	5
	none	minimal	some	moderate	significant
Weekly Impact	1	2	3	4	5

Check the Feeling Wheel inside the front cover and list any emotion(s) you are feeling.

Module 5

WEEK 5.4: Evaluating

|||||||||||||||||||||||||||||||||||||||||||||||||||||||||||||||||||||||||||||||||||||||||||||||||||||||||||||||||||||||||||||||||||||

The previous week's skill, solving problems, leads right into this week's responsible decision-making skill: Evaluating. After you've solved a problem, your decision-making work is not complete. You need to continue to monitor the situation and evaluate if your solution was effective. We're not suggesting that every decision you make in a day deserves the same amount of evaluation. Still, big, important decisions like dealing with student crisis or deciding on curriculum changes deserve the time to know if the solution is having its intended effect.

All evaluation begins with a set of criteria by which you can judge effectiveness. So how might you define an effective decision? You can ask yourself the following questions as you examine your decision-making process and the consequences of the decision:

- Did I make the decision deliberately and thoughtfully?

- Did I consider all vital information and factors? Did I listen to others and consider their values and beliefs?

- Did I consider my values and beliefs? Was I biased in any way?

- Was the decision communicated well?

- Who is benefitting from the decision?

- Is the decision causing any unintended consequences?

This week as you go about your decision-making responsibilities, think about which decisions need evaluating, which values and beliefs you rely on most to make those decisions, and the consequences of these decisions.

We also want to point out that you might wish to move back and forth between this skill and the synergistic skills **1.2 Strengths of Emotions and 2.2 Goal Setting and Productive Habits.**

5.4 DAY 1: Evaluating

☆ *"The risk of a wrong decision is preferable to the terror of indecision."* —Maimonides

Reflection for Today: Do you agree or disagree with this quote? Do you delay decision making because you are afraid of making the wrong choice?

_____

_____

_____

_____

_____

List one thing you're grateful for today:

_____

Check the Feeling Wheel inside the front cover and list any emotion(s) you are feeling.

5.4 DAY 2: Evaluating

 "Let me tell you, if you're ever making a decision and the principle reason you'll do it is because of money, then it is absolutely the incorrect decision."
—Hill Harper

Reflection for Today: Although you may not make decisions based on money, what principles, values, and beliefs guide most of your choices? Are those working for you and your school?

_____

_____

_____

_____

List one thing you're grateful for today:

_____

Check the Feeling Wheel inside the front cover and list any emotion(s) you are feeling.

5.4 DAY 3: Evaluating

⭐ *"I always go back to Harry Truman: Should we drop an atomic bomb to save 100,000 lives? That's a hell of a decision to make. Did he make that decision by himself? No, he had advisers."* —Lee Iacocca

Practice for Today: Think about a significant decision you recently made. Find two or three people whom you trust the most in your school and ask them about the consequences of that decision.

_____

_____

_____

_____

List one thing you're grateful for today:

_____

Check the Feeling Wheel inside the front cover and list any emotion(s) you are feeling.

5.4 DAY 4: Evaluating

 "Democracy requires information. Plato knew that informed decision-making requires knowledge."
—Mary Beard

Practice for Today: Are you considering the best information and knowledge to make your decisions? As you make decisions today, try to obtain twice as much information as you usually do or talk to somebody with lots of knowledge about your decision.

List one thing you're grateful for today:

Check the Feeling Wheel inside the front cover and list any emotion(s) you are feeling.

5.4 DAY 5: Evaluating

☆ *"An expert is someone who has succeeded in making decisions and judgements simpler through knowing what to pay attention to and what to ignore."* —Edward de Bono

Leadership Considerations: This week, you considered how to evaluate the decisions you make in your role as a leader in your school. As you end this week, consider the following questions:

1. Are you becoming an expert in decision making and in evaluating the impact of your decisions? What are you paying the most attention to when making your decisions?

2. What questions do you need to consider more in evaluating your decisions?

3. Review all the notes you took this week and find your one best thought. Now go share your insight with somebody who might benefit from it.

Weekly Effort	1	2	3	4	5
	none	minimal	some	moderate	significant

Weekly Impact	1	2	3	4	5

Check the Feeling Wheel inside the front cover and list any emotion(s) you are feeling.

Module 5

WEEK 5.5: Reflecting

|||||||||||||||||||||||||||||||||||||||||||||||||||||||||||||||||||||||||||||||||||||||||||||||||||||||||||||||||||||||||||||||||||||||||||||

Once you've made a decision, carried it out, and evaluated it, your next task is to reflect on the process and learn from it. Reflection remains a critical but often ignored aspect of leadership and can lead to a deeper and more nuanced degree of self-awareness.

Reflection suggests taking time to contemplate your decisions, how you made them, and what you learned about the consequences of your decisions. Reflection requires taking a neutral stance toward yourself and stepping outside of the situation to reflect on it with honesty. Although carving out time to reflect on your decisions requires hard-to-find time during your day (or night!), interrogating your decision making leads to greater wisdom about yourself and others.

This week, you'll reflect on reflecting. Consider your skills, awareness of your own emotions and values, and awareness of others' feelings and values during your decision-making process.

We also want to point out that you might wish to move back and forth between this skill and the synergistic skills **1.1 Developing Accurate Self-Perception, 1.2 Strengths of Emotions, and 2.2 Goal Setting and Productive Habits.**

Module 5

5.5 DAY 1: Reflecting

☆ *"By three methods we may learn wisdom: First, by reflection, which is noblest; second, by imitation, which is easiest; and third by experience, which is the bitterest."* —Confucius

Reflection for Today: How much reflection do you do on your decision making? Would you benefit from scheduling time to reflect on your day or week? Why or why not?

_____

_____

_____

_____

List one thing you're grateful for today:

_____

Check the Feeling Wheel inside the front cover and list any emotion(s) you are feeling.

5.5 DAY 2: Reflecting

☆ *"Follow effective action with quiet reflection. From the quiet reflection will come even more effective action."* —Peter Drucker

Reflection for Today: Why do you think reflection will lead to more effective action? How might your decision making improve with better reflection?

_____

_____

_____

_____

_____

List one thing you're grateful for today:

_____

Check the Feeling Wheel inside the front cover and list any emotion(s) you are feeling.

Module 5

5.5 DAY 3: Reflecting

⭐ *"Without reflection, we go blindly on our way, creating more unintended consequences, and failing to achieve anything useful."* —Margaret J. Wheatley

Practice for Today: Find five minutes today to reflect on a decision you have made recently. Think about how you made the decision and your emotions and values in the decision.

_____

_____

_____

_____

List one thing you're grateful for today:

_____

Check the Feeling Wheel inside the front cover and list any emotion(s) you are feeling.

5.5 DAY 4: Reflecting

☆ *"Change comes from reflection."* —Genesis P-Orridge

Practice for Today: What is one change you need to make in your decision making? Why? Start working on that today.

_____

_____

_____

_____

_____

_____

_____

List one thing you're grateful for today:

_____

Check the Feeling Wheel inside the front cover and list any emotion(s) you are feeling.

Module 5

5.5 DAY 5: Reflecting

☆ *"Most executives I know are so action-oriented, or action-addicted, that time for reflection is the first casualty of their success."* —Margaret Heffernan

Leadership Considerations: This week, you considered the importance of reflection in developing wisdom and more self-awareness as a leader in your school. As you end this week, consider the following questions:

1. Are you too action-oriented at the expense of reflection and growth? How can you slow down and take more time for self-reflection?

2. How can you become more aware of yourself during decision making? How can you become more aware of others during decision making?

3. Review all the notes you took this week and find your one best thought. Now go share your insight with somebody who might benefit from it.

Weekly Effort	1	2	3	4	5
	none	minimal	some	moderate	significant

Weekly Impact	1	2	3	4	5

Check the Feeling Wheel inside the front cover and list any emotion(s) you are feeling.

Module 5

WEEK 5.6: Ethical Responsibility

At the start of every school year, teachers and students across the country engage in a conversation about ethical responsibility. More commonly known as *Classroom Rules, Agreements,* or *Our Commitments,* class communities discuss what it means to be ethically responsible to oneself and each other as a member of a learning community.

As a leader, some of the definition of ethical responsibility is taken care of for you. If you suspect a student is suffering abuse at home, you are both ethically and legally required to report your concern to Child Protective Services. Your school is governed by federal, state, and local laws that require you to provide specific services to specific subgroups of students. To demonstrate ethical responsibility, you need to have a clear understanding of what acting ethically means to your community and to you.

In addition to laws that, at least to some degree, specify what it means to be ethically responsible, perhaps you also establish norms with your staff. Such statements seek to guide your interactions with each other, setting expectations for what each member can expect of another. Or maybe your community and you create a culture of ethical responsibility through other means, such as raising community member examples of what ethical responsibility looks like.

Without such a moral compass, it is impossible to determine whether or not anyone, including you, in the community demonstrates ethical responsibility, which is especially relevant to responsible decision making. Why? Because decision making is the moment in which power gets exercised. For the good of the entire community, you, as the leader, need to give the community every reason to believe that you value ethical responsibility as part of your decision-making practice.

> **Decision making is the moment in which power gets exercised.**

This week, you'll have opportunities to reflect on how ethical responsibility shows up (or maybe it doesn't yet) in your leadership practice. We also want to point out that you might wish to move back and forth between this skill and the synergistic skills **3.3 Appreciating Diversity, 3.4 Respect for Others, and 4.3 Relationship Building.**

5.6 DAY 1: Ethical Responsibility

☆ *"Before I can live with other folks, I've got to live with myself. The one thing that doesn't abide by majority rule is a person's conscience."* —Harper Lee

Reflection for Today: Do you have an educational moral code? Have you ever given yourself the time to imagine what that might look like for you? Take some time today to reflect on either what a new or revised educational moral code might look like for your practice.

_____

_____

_____

_____

_____

List one thing you're grateful for today:

_____

Check the Feeling Wheel inside the front cover and list any emotion(s) you are feeling.

5.6 DAY 2: Ethical Responsibility

 "Even the most rational approach to ethics is defenseless if there isn't the will to do what is right."
—Alexander Solzhenitsyn

Reflection for Today: Are there times during the day, week, month, and year when you find that you have more energy? What might your calendar look like if you align when you have the most energy to make your most impactful decisions to ensure maximum ethical responsibility when making those decisions?

_____

_____

_____

_____

List one thing you're grateful for today:

_____

Check the Feeling Wheel inside the front cover and list any emotion(s) you are feeling.

5.6 DAY 3: Ethical Responsibility

☆ *"The ultimate measure of a man is not where he stands in moments of comfort and convenience, but where he stands at times of challenge and controversy."* —Martin Luther King, Jr.

Practice for Today: Is there an ethical but difficult decision you've been putting off? If so, try to make that decision today.

List one thing you're grateful for today:

Check the Feeling Wheel inside the front cover and list any emotion(s) you are feeling.

5.6 DAY 4: Ethical Responsibility

⟨☆⟩ *"I have learned over the years that when one's mind is made up, this diminishes fear; knowing what must be done does away with fear."* —Rosa Parks

Practice for Today: Today, try to add to the knowledge you are gathering around making a particular decision. Try to reduce any fear you may have related to this decision by learning more about what you will need to make the decision.

_____

_____

_____

_____

_____

List one thing you're grateful for today:

_____

Check the Feeling Wheel inside the front cover and list any emotion(s) you are feeling.

5.6 DAY 5: Ethical Responsibility

⭐ *"I'd prefer to be true to myself, even at the hazard of incurring the ridicule of others, rather than to be false, and to incur my own abhorrence."* —Frederick Douglass

Leadership Considerations: This week, you contemplated the notion of ethical responsibility as an aspect of your decision-making processes. As you end this week, consider the following questions:

1. How often are you true to your sense of ethics when you make decisions for your school?
2. Does fear of what others may think about your decisions limit the frequency with which you make ethically responsible decisions? Might you be able to identify one action you could take to reduce that fear?
3. Review all the notes you took this week and find your one best thought. Now go share your insight with somebody who might benefit from it.

Weekly Effort

1	2	3	4	5
none	minimal	some	moderate	significant

Weekly Impact

1	2	3	4	5

Check the Feeling Wheel inside the front cover and list any emotion(s) you are feeling.

Module 5

Reflection and Action Planning

1. What do you see as the key ideas to continue to think and learn about in this module?

2. Are there any skills from the diagnostic or your initial practice attempts you want to keep working on? If you haven't done so already, add the skill to your action plan.

Module Effort	1	2	3	4	5
	none	minimal	some	moderate	significant

Module Impact	1	2	3	4	5

Check the Feeling Wheel inside the front cover and list any emotion(s) you are feeling.

MODULE 6: NEXT STEPS

In the introduction to this book, we explain a brief framework about the paths by which a leader can impact student achievement (Leithwood, Anderson, Mascall, & Strauss, 2010). As a brief reminder, those paths include:

- The Rational path that includes the technical core of curriculum, teaching, and learning

- The Organizational path that provides for structures, policies, standard operating procedures and culture

- The Family path that includes how a school includes and works with parents and the community

- The Emotional path that directs an individuals' attention, cognition, and perceptions

In particular, we noted over the past 20 years of reform in U.S. schools the prevailing use of the rational and organizational paths for improving achievement in academic areas. To summarize, focusing primarily on these paths often failed to account for the immense, negative consequences these efforts had on the emotional states of leaders and teachers (Leithwood & Beatty, 2008). Stress, burnout, and attrition have become the *de facto* state for many educators during this era (Carver-Thomas & Darling-Hammond, 2017). With that state of affairs in mind, we also stressed that if you focus on social and emotional learning for yourself, you will impact your teachers on a profoundly human level. The goal of this book has been to support you in driving that positive impact.

As you worked through the modules and daily prompts, practicing these skills, we hope you have seen the necessity of this deep work for evolving as a leader. You likely found this deep work challenging at times. Any time we try to change ourselves in any way, we often fall short of our intent. We set a goal; we don't see the success we think we should, get discouraged, and give up. Instead of embracing risk and failure, we aim for comfort and what we know. But consider two thoughts: First, any stress you put on your social-emotional system to improve will help your leadership grow. Expect, and even seek in some cases, that stress and those failures. Learn to embrace risk and discomfort. We tell our students to embrace these experiences, yet we too infrequently model those very behaviors in our practice.

Second, the world needs you to develop your SEL skills now more than ever. With many new challenges in our society, technological advances, and an increased need to focus intently on equity in all our schools, prioritizing investment in your leadership development is not just essential; it may very well be existential for some members of your community. You trained to understand how schools work, how budgets work, and how teaching and learning work. Yet few school leaders prepare to understand what drives individuals or groups to engage in the difficult task of teaching and improving schools. These social and emotional skills, however, form the very foundation of your leadership. If that foundation is not secure and steady, then all other aspects of your practice rest on shaky ground. No matter how technically strong you may be in other areas, without a sophisticated social and emotional base, it will be challenging to be the type of leader you can be and who your community needs you to be.

In the book, *The Obstacle is the Way* (2014), author Ryan Holiday describes how all leaders face a variety of challenges that frequently limit their impact. Often, that obstacle is ourselves—our inability to understand our triggers, our inability to control our tempers or our speech, our failure to listen deeply to others, or our inability to see ourselves clearly so that we may see others clearly. These are all obstacles that can interfere with our ability to lead and to influence and impact the lives of others.

Holiday quotes the famous Roman general Marcus Aurelius who understood these obstacles close to 2,000 years ago by writing:

The impediment to action advances action.

What stands in the way becomes the way.

In essence, what Marcus Aurelius concludes is that the obstacles we face when dealing with our emotions and relationships with others are opportunities to practice and get better at leadership itself. Schools are nothing if not a town square teeming with social and emotional interactions every day, and you are constantly tested. Are you kind and virtuous? Are you growing as you ask others to grow? Are you deeply hearing others? Are you developing effective and impactful relationships with others and helping your teams develop? And in the end, can you say that you mattered to your staff and students because of who you were as a person? These are the tests that matter, and we hope these ideas prompted valuable practice opportunities to prepare for these tests.

Final Thoughts and Reflections

In the end, we hope you take to heart our core messages regarding the social and emotional competencies discussed throughout this book:

- See self-awareness as an accurate portrayal of yourself
- See self-management as the control of your inner life

- See social-awareness as attunement to others

- See relationship skills as the continual building of trust

- See responsible decision making as sharing values and power with others

- Overall, see SEL as your key to better leadership

By using these simple insights and revisiting some of your favorite prompts and ideas, you can continue to develop your SEL skills. Moreover, you can begin to work with your leadership team or other teams to help them grow their SEL skills. How might you continue to learn and grow, and how might you help others do the same? Let's review the simple theory of action we laid out in the introduction and start thinking about how the ideas presented in the previous five modules could begin to influence teams or a whole school.

- If we (teams or whole school) use the resources (the book, additional resources, deliberate practice plan), and

- If we engage in the suggested activities (daily prompts and practice, note taking and reflections, conversations with others), then

- As educators, we will have
    - Increased our awareness of high-level SEL concepts
    - Increased our understanding of macro- and micro-skills
    - Developed a more detailed self-assessment of our SEL proficiency
    - Developed more awareness of opportunities and threats in our leadership
    - Developed an enhanced practice habit for SEL skills

- And we will have started to create these impacts
    - Stronger relationships with each other to increase engagement and retention
    - Stronger relationships with families and community to increase inclusivity
    - More awareness of inequities
    - Better mental and physical health for ourselves
    - Increased credibility for using SEL initiatives
    - Increased opportunities to scale SEL implementation across our school

As you use this theory of action, be patient with yourself and others; be consistent. Use this book as often as you need; we designed it to support your work every

Figure 6.1 Team Theory of Action

If teams use these resources . . .	**. . . and engage in these activities . . .**	**. . . they should develop these skills . . .**	**. . . and create these impacts.**
The Daily SEL Leader Book	Engagement/ reflection on daily prompts	Increased awareness of high-level SEL concepts	Stronger relationships with each other, leading to increased engagement and retention
Suggested additional readings	Note taking based on engagement with daily prompts	Increased understanding of macro and micro SEL skills	Stronger relationships with families and community, leading to more inclusive learning cultures
Their time, to reflect and take notes	Conversation with others re: self-observations driven by the daily prompts	More detailed self-assessment of their SEL proficiency	Recognition of inequitable school conditions
Their previous leadership experience		Increased awareness of opportunities and threats based on more detailed self-assessment	Increases in your mental and physical health
Their previous SEL experience		Increased practice on SEL topics most relevant to them	Increases in your credibility when leading SEL initiatives
			More opportunities to scale SEL skills implementation at your school

Inputs	**Activities**	**Outcomes**	**Impact**

Source: Gears by rambo182/iStock.com; Clapper Board by Katsiaryna Pleshakova/iStock.com; Graph by rambo182/iStock.com; and Star by Katsiaryna Pleshakova/iStock.com.

school year. No one masters even one of these skills in a short amount of time. Now that you've reached the end of the book, take action right now. Write down the answers to the three final reflection questions, and set aside time to revise and update your action plan. Make a commitment to yourself and your students to do this work every day, no matter how small the scale, then start working with other leaders in your school.

Every minute you invest in yourself, you invest in the future of your students, families, and staff, as well. No matter how scarce your school's resources are, the only person who can keep you from doing this work is you. For the good of your community, we hope that you will not let that happen and that we can support you in some small way to become even better, healthier, and more resilient than you already are. As you can see, what started with you as a school leader can now ripple across many other lives in your community. It begins with you.

With that in mind, here is your final quote and reflection.

> *"The obstacle in the path becomes the path. Never forget, within every obstacle is an opportunity to improve our condition."*
>
> —Ryan Holiday

1. Throughout the book, what did you find most surprising or interesting about yourself?

2. What are the obstacles you face in strengthening your social and emotional skills? What is your plan to overcome these obstacles?

3. What is holding you back from pursuing and developing better social and emotional skills?

APPENDIX A

||||||||||||||||||||||||||||||||||||||||||||||||||||||||||||||||||||||||||||||||||||||||||||||||||||||||||

Daily SEL for Leaders Diagnostic

Directions: This diagnostic provides you with an opportunity to illuminate a more in-depth understanding of your social-emotional skills. Each competency is organized into discrete skills, and each skill asks you to provide a rating, from Strongly Disagree to Strongly Agree, for three statements. After rating each of the three specific statements for each skill, add up your ratings (e.g., 2 + 4 + 3), divide them by three, and enter your result in the space provided for each skill. Repeat this process for each skill in each competency. This rating gives you a comparison of your skills within the competency. When you have determined your average score for each skill, add up your average scores and then divide by the total number of skills in each competency (we've provided you with the total) to reveal your score for the full competency. Once you've found your average for each competency, you'll be able to compare your ratings across competencies and use them to develop an action plan.

1. Self-Awareness: The ability to accurately recognize one's own emotions, thoughts, and values and how they influence behavior. The ability to accurately assess one's strengths and limitations, with a well-grounded sense of confidence, optimism, and a growth mindset.	1 Strongly Disagree	2 Disagree	3 Unsure	4 Agree	5 Strongly Agree
1.1 Identifying Emotions					
1. I routinely recognize when I feel my emotions change.	1	2	3	4	5
2. I can easily identify and name the emotions I am feeling.	1	2	3	4	5
3. I can easily distinguish between strong and weak emotions.	1	2	3	4	5
Average: Add all/3 = _____					

(Continued)

(Continued)

1.2 Accurate Self-Perception					
1. My perceptions about myself match those of others.	1	2	3	4	5
2. I have a good sense of who I am.	1	2	3	4	5
3. I am honest with myself about my shortcomings.	1	2	3	4	5
	Average: Add all/3 = _____				
1.3 Recognizing Strengths					
1. I feel I have internal strength to get me through challenges.	1	2	3	4	5
2. I am very clear about what I am good at.	1	2	3	4	5
3. I can accurately judge which aspects of my leadership practice I need to grow.	1	2	3	4	5
	Average: Add all/3 = _____				
1.4 Self-Confidence					
1. I try to stay humble even though I feel I have several good qualities.	1	2	3	4	5
2. I feel I do many things well, or at least as well as others in my role.	1	2	3	4	5
3. I feel people believe in me because of my confidence.	1	2	3	4	5
	Average: Add all/3 = _____				
1.5 Self-Efficacy					
1. When facing difficult times, I am certain that I will accomplish my goal.	1	2	3	4	5

2. I am able to achieve most of the goals I set for myself.	1	2	3	4	5
3. I am able to successfully overcome many challenges.	1	2	3	4	5
	Average: Add all/3 = _____				
Self-Awareness Total	**Add all/15 =** _____				

2. Self-Management: The ability to successfully regulate one's emotions, thoughts, and behaviors in different situations— effectively managing stress, controlling impulses, and motivating oneself. The ability to set and work toward personal and academic goals.	1 Strongly Disagree	2 Disagree	3 Unsure	4 Agree	5 Strongly Agree
2.1 Self-Motivation					
1. I have a mindset that welcomes challenging situations as an opportunity to learn and grow.	1	2	3	4	5
2. I can easily motivate myself to meet new challenges.	1	2	3	4	5
3. I am always looking for experiences that challenge me.	1	2	3	4	5
	Average: Add all/3 = _____				
2.2 Goal Setting and Productive Habits					
1. I have a mindset that focuses on setting goals for myself.	1	2	3	4	5
2. I frequently monitor if I am making progress toward my goals.	1	2	3	4	5
3. I can easily adjust my goals when necessary.	1	2	3	4	5
	Average: Add all/3 = _____				

(Continued)

Appendix A: Daily SEL for Leaders Diagnostic ■ 205

(Continued)

2.3 Organizational Skills					
1. I believe that being highly organized saves time and effort.	1	2	3	4	5
2. I use effective systems to help me be more productive.	1	2	3	4	5
3. I rarely struggle with meeting deadlines.	1	2	3	4	5
	Average: Add all/3 = _____				
2.4 Impulse Control					
1. I can easily feel my emotions growing.	1	2	3	4	5
2. I have strategies to control my emotions when I feel them intensifying.	1	2	3	4	5
3. I typically don't say things in the moment that I regret later.	1	2	3	4	5
	Average: Add all/3 = _____				
2.5 Stress Management					
1. I can easily feel my levels of stress.	1	2	3	4	5
2. I regularly assess my stress level.	1	2	3	4	5
3. Even though I give a lot to others, I know when to recharge.	1	2	3	4	5
	Average: Add all/3 = _____				
2.6 Self-Discipline					
1. I can easily concentrate with distractions going on.	1	2	3	4	5
2. I can easily control my impulses.	1	2	3	4	5
3. I can usually stick to goals I set long term.	1	2	3	4	5
	Average: Add all/3 = _____				
Self-Awareness Total	Add all/18 = _____				

3. Social Awareness: The ability to take the perspective of and empathize with others, including those from diverse backgrounds and cultures. The ability to understand social and ethical norms for behavior and to recognize family, school, and community resources and supports.	1 Strongly Disagree	2 Disagree	3 Unsure	4 Agree	5 Strongly Agree
3.1 Perspective Taking					
1. I believe it is important to consider others' perspectives before sharing my own.	1	2	3	4	5
2. I can easily understand an issue from another point of view.	1	2	3	4	5
3. I frequently leave a conversation feeling we understood each other's perspectives.	1	2	3	4	5
	Average: Add all/3 = _____				
3.2 Empathy					
1. I am often curious about the feelings of others.	1	2	3	4	5
2. I can often tell how people feel without them having to say anything.	1	2	3	4	5
3. My feelings often mirror those of others.	1	2	3	4	5
	Average: Add all/3 = _____				
3.3 Appreciating Diversity					
1. I always want to gain an understanding of the lives of people from diverse backgrounds.	1	2	3	4	5

(Continued)

(Continued)

2. I find it easy to relate to people from different races and cultures.	1	2	3	4	5
3. Understanding people from different races and cultures allows for a richer experience.	1	2	3	4	5
Source: Adapted from Appreciation of Diversity Scale. https://www.okhighered.org/ okcampuscompact/pdf/2019 tmce-diversity-appreciation-scale .pdf	**Average: Add all/3 =** _____				
3.4 Respect for Others					
1. I prioritize listening to others.	1	2	3	4	5
2. I do not criticize people openly.	1	2	3	4	5
3. I allow people the freedom to express their thoughts and opinions.	**Average: Add all/3 =** _____				
Social Awareness Total	**Add all/12 =** _____				

4. Relationship Skills: The ability to establish and maintain healthy and rewarding relationships with diverse individuals and groups. The ability to communicate clearly, listen well, cooperate with others, resist inappropriate social pressure, negotiate conflict constructively, and seek and offer help when needed.	1 **Strongly Disagree**	2 **Disagree**	3 **Unsure**	4 **Agree**	5 **Strongly Agree**

4.1 Communication					
1. I believe in integrating diverse voices from my community when communicating.	1	2	3	4	5
2. I work to make my communication constructive and optimistic.	1	2	3	4	5
3. People appreciate the clarity of my message when I speak.	1	2	3	4	5
	Average: Add all/3 = _____				
4.2 Social Engagement					
1. I believe strongly in engaging people on a personal and professional level.	1	2	3	4	5
2. I use different ways to engage diverse groups.	1	2	3	4	5
3. I easily engage with different groups.	1	2	3	4	5
	Average: Add all/3 = _____				
4.3 Relationship Building					
1. I believe that all members of my school community have something positive to offer.	1	2	3	4	5
2. I easily negotiate conflict in my relationships.	1	2	3	4	5
3. I can easily build relationships with different groups and people.	1	2	3	4	5
	Average: Add all/3 = _____				

(Continued)

(Continued)

4.4 Teamwork					
1. I strongly believe that learning from each other makes the most effective team.	1	2	3	4	5
2. I work to leverage people's strengths on teams.	1	2	3	4	5
3. Teams I lead feel that they can share and make mistakes without fear.	1	2	3	4	5
	Average: Add all/3 = _____				
Relationship Skills Total	**Add all/12** = _____				

5. Responsible Decision Making: The ability to make constructive choices about personal behavior and social interactions based on ethical standards, safety concerns, and social norms. The realistic evaluation of consequences of various actions, and a consideration of the well-being of oneself and others.	1 Strongly Disagree	2 Disagree	3 Unsure	4 Agree	5 Strongly Agree
5.1 Identifying Problems					
1. I can easily anticipate problems that may occur in social interactions.	1	2	3	4	5
2. I use concrete strategies to assess root causes.	1	2	3	4	5
3. I can easily determine the problems affecting my well-being.	1	2	3	4	5
	Average: Add all/3 = _____				

5.2 Analyzing Situations					
1. I can easily recognize how my own emotions impact my analysis of situations.	1	2	3	4	5
2. I always try to gather the most information I can about situations.	1	2	3	4	5
3. I have a process by which I analyze situations.	1	2	3	4	5
	Average: Add all/3 = _____				

5.3 Solving Problems					
1. I feel I take enough time to solve problems well so they don't resurface.	1	2	3	4	5
2. I always consider multiple options before deciding on an ultimate solution.	1	2	3	4	5
3. My solutions to problems usually work out well.	1	2	3	4	5
	Average: Add all/3 = _____				

5.4 Evaluating					
1. I believe that I need to set criteria by which to evaluate my decisions.	1	2	3	4	5
2. I frequently evaluate the impact of my decision making.	1	2	3	4	5
3. I learn to make better decisions by evaluating their impact.	1	2	3	4	5
	Average: Add all/3 = _____				

(Continued)

(Continued)

5.5 Reflecting					
1. My mindset is to try to learn from the decisions I make.	1	2	3	4	5
2. I frequently reflect about the process and outcomes of the decisions I make.	1	2	3	4	5
3. I frequently consider how my own emotions and relationships influence my decisions.	1	2	3	4	5
	Average: Add all/3 = _____				
5.6 Ethical Responsibility					
1. I have a set of clearly articulated values by which I make decisions.	1	2	3	4	5
2. I frequently consider my values when I make decisions.	1	2	3	4	5
3. I can easily stand by my decisions because of my values.	1	2	3	4	5
	Average: Add all/3 = _____				
Responsible Decision Making Total	**Add all/18 =** _____				

APPENDIX B

||||||||||||||||||||||||||||||||||||||||||||||||||||||||||||||||||||||||||||||||||||||||||||||||||||||||||||||||||||||||||||||||||||

Daily SEL for Leaders Practice Plan

Directions: This appendix and the options presented below will help you better engage with the content and develop the skills you choose through practice. Like any other skill, developing a social-emotional skill requires an ongoing and deliberate practice routine to improve. Experts in this area suggest only "the right sort of practice carried out over a sufficient period of time leads to improvement. Nothing else" (Ericsson & Poole, 2017).

Deliberate practice is based on four basic steps that will help guide how you develop your plan.

1. **Set a clear specific mini goal** in service of a more extensive performance.

2. **Focus your practice** by setting reminders of the goal and working on it with deliberate intention.

3. **Set up a feedback system**. People do not improve performance without extensive feedback. Feedback helps narrow the gap between where the skill is and where it could be.

4. **Get out of the comfort zone**. To get better, people need to get out of their most comfortable routines and move to the edge of their competence. Human performance does not change all at once but needs a constant push for improvement.

Setting Up Your Practice Plan

Since there are multiple ways to progress through the book based on need, we offer five different options to help you develop your deliberate practice plan using the form below.

Option 1: Start With the Diagnostic

After reading the introduction, take the diagnostic and determine two or three primary skills to focus on and read through those sections.

Option 2: Start at the Beginning

If you choose to read the book module by module, you can identify certain skills per module that you wish to work on.

Option 3: Choose a Path

Since so many of the skills in the book are interrelated, we've compiled five different paths, each with a specific theme. You can choose one or more of the paths and list the specific skills you want to practice and develop. These paths are listed in the Introduction, in Figure 0.4.

Option 4: Create a Path

Using the results from the diagnostic or skills that are of most interest to you, choose some and practice those you want to develop.

Option 5: Choose a Focus

Choose one module or one skill for a longer period of time and determine how to practice more in-depth over a longer period of time.

Figure B.1 Model of a Practice Plan

Module	Which skill(s) and/or week do you want to develop? (these are your mini-goals)	What is your plan for practicing this skill? (this is how you will focus your practice and get out of your comfort zone)	How frequently will you practice this skill?	How will you set up your feedback system to know if you are improving?
2- Self-Management	**My goal is to improve my** *Impulse Control* *Week 2, 4*	1. Notice what triggers me 2. Notice in meetings when I feel impulses to show anger and speak out 3. Breathe in the moment 4. Slow my processing down 5. Only speak when I feel calm	Week 1: daily individual interactions Week 2: 1–2 meetings Week 3: 2–3 meetings Week 4: all meetings	1. Let staff know my goal 2. Track my impulse to anger and speaking over four weeks 3. By Week 3 ask at end of meetings if my tone was appropriate

Figure B.2 Practice Plan #1

Module	Which skill(s) and/or week do you want to develop? (these are your mini-goals)	What is your plan for practicing this skill? (this is how you will focus your practice and get out of your comfort zone)	How frequently will you practice this skill?	How will you set up your feedback system to know if you are improving?

Figure B.3 Practice Plan #2

Module	Which skill(s) and/or week do you want to develop? (these are your mini-goals)	What is your plan for practicing this skill? (this is how you will focus your practice and get out of your comfort zone)	How frequently will you practice this skill?	How will you set up your feedback system to know if you are improving?

REFERENCES

American Federation of Teachers. (2017). *Educators Quality of Life Survey*. https://www .aft.org/sites/default/files/2017_eqwl_survey_web.pdf

American Psychological Association. (n.d.). Self-discipline. *APA Dictionary of Psychology*. Washington, DC: Author. https://dictionary.apa.org/self-discipline

Berlin, H. A., & Hollander, E. (2008). Understanding the differences between impulsivity and compulsivity. *Psychiatric Times, 25*(8). https://www.psychiatrictimes.com/impulse-control-disorders/understanding-differences-between-impulsivity-and-compulsivity

Brackett, M. (2018). *Permission to feel: Unlocking the power of emotions to help our kids, ourselves, and our society thrive.* Celadon Books.

Browning, L. D., Morris, G. H., & Kee, K. F. (2011). The role of communication in positive organizational scholarship. In K. Cameron & G. Spreitzer (Eds.), *Handbook of positive organizational scholarship* (pp. 566–578). Oxford University Press.

Carver-Thomas, D., & Darling-Hammond, L. (2017). *Teacher turnover: Why it matters and what we can do about it.* Learning Policy Institute.

CASEL Framework. (n.d.). SEL: What are the core competence areas and where are they promoted? https://casel.org/core-competencies/

Clear, J. (2019). *Atomic habits: An easy & proven way to build good habits & break bad ones.* Avery.

Clifton, J., & Harter, J. (2019). *It's the manager.* Gallup Press.

Edmondson, A. (2014). *Teaming: How organizations learn, innovate, and compete in the knowledge economy.* Jossey-Bass.

Ericsson, A., & Pool, R. (2016). *Peak: Secrets from the new science of expertise.* Eamon Dolan/ Houghton Mifflin Harcourt.

Evenden, J. L. (1999). Varieties of impulsivity. *Psychopharmacology, 146*, 348–361. https:// doi.org/10.1007/PL00005481

Feldman Barrett, L. (2019). *How emotions are made: The secret life of the brain.* Mariner Books.

Goleman, D. (2006). *Social intelligence: The new science of human relationships.* Bantam Books.

Goleman, D. (2005). *Emotional intelligence: Why it can matter more than IQ.* Bantam.

Hattie, J. (2012). *Visible learning for teachers.* Routledge.

Holiday, R. (2014). *The obstacle is the way.* Profile Books.

Kahneman, D. (2011). *Thinking fast and slow.* Farrar, Strauss and Giroux.

Knoblach, S. (2019). Employee engagement benchmarking study. Herndon, VA: K12 Insight. https://www.k12insight.com/resources/#benchmark

Leithwood, K., & Beatty, B. (2008). *Leading with teacher emotions in mind.* Corwin.

Leithwood, K., & Seashore-Louis, K. (2012). *Linking leadership to student learning.* Jossey Bass.

Leithwood, K., Anderson, S. E., Mascall, B., & Strauss, T. (2010). School leaders' influences on student learning: The four paths. In T. Bush, L. Bell, & D. Middlewood (Eds.), *The principles of educational leadership & management* (2nd ed., pp. 13–30). SAGE.

Leithwood, K., Sun, J., & Pollock, K. (Eds.). (2017). *How school leaders contribute to student success: The four paths framework.* Springer.

Mayo Clinic. (2014, April 14). *Stress symptoms: Effects on your body and behavior.* https://www.mayoclinic.org/healthy-lifestyle/stress-management/in-depth/stress-symptoms/art-20050987

Muraven, M., & Baumeister, R. F. (2000). Self-regulation and depletion of limited resources: Does self-control resemble a muscle? *Psychological Bulletin, 126*(2), 247–259. doi:10.1037/0033-2909.126.2.247

National Center for Education Statistics. (2020). *Characteristics of public school principals.* https://nces.ed.gov/programs/coe/indicator_cls.asp#:~:text=In%202017%E2%80%9318%2C%20about%2078,and%209%20percent%20were%20Hispanic

Page, S. (2020, May 26). Back to school? 1 in 5 teachers are unlikely to return to reopened classrooms this fall, poll says. *USA Today.* https://www.usatoday.com/story/news/education/2020/05/26/coronavirus-schools-teachers-poll-ipsos-parents-fall-online/5254729002/

Ryan, R. M., & Deci, E. L. (2017). *Self-determination theory: Basic psychological needs in motivation, development, and wellness.* Guilford Press.

Schunk, D. H. (1990). Goal setting and self-efficacy during self-regulated learning. *Educational Psychologist, 25,* 71–86. https://libres.uncg.edu/ir/uncg/f/D_Schunk_Goal_1990.pdf

Peterson, C., & Seligman, M. (2004). *Character strengths and virtues.* Oxford University Press.

Zabrowski, Z., & Slaski, S. (2003). Content and forms of theory of self-awareness. *Imagination, Cognition, and Personality, 23*(2&3), 99–119.

Leadership That Makes an Impact

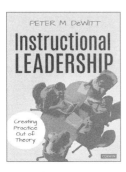

PETER M. DEWITT

This step-by-step how-to guide presents the six driving forces of instructional leadership within a multistage model for implementation, delivering lasting improvement through small collaborative changes.

JOHN HATTIE & RAYMOND L. SMITH

Based on the most current Visible Learning® research with contributions from education thought leaders around the world, this book includes practical ideas for leaders to implement high-impact strategies to strengthen entire school cultures and advocate for all students.

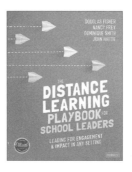

DOUGLAS FISHER, NANCY FREY, DOMINIQUE SMITH, & JOHN HATTIE

The essential hands-on resource offers guidance on leading school and school systems from a distance and delivering on the promise of equitable, quality learning experiences for students.

STEVEN M. CONSTANTINO

Explore the how-to's of establishing family empowerment through building trust, and reflect on implicit bias, equitable learning outcomes, and the role family engagement plays.

MICHAEL FULLAN, JOANNE QUINN, & JOANNE MCEACHEN

The comprehensive strategy of deep learning incorporates practical tools and processes to engage educational stakeholders in new partnerships, mobilize whole-system change, and transform learning for all students.

JOANNE QUINN, JOANNE MCEACHEN, MICHAEL FULLAN, MAG GARDNER, & MAX DRUMMY

Dive into deep learning with this hands-on guide to creating learning experiences that give purpose, unleash student potential, and transform not only learning, but life itself.

DAVIS CAMPBELL & MICHAEL FULLAN

The model outlined in this book develops a systems approach to governing local schools collaboratively to become exemplars of highly effective decision making, leadership, and action.

DAVIS CAMPBELL, MICHAEL FULLAN, BABS KAVANAUGH, & ELEANOR ADAM

As a supplement to the best-selling *The Governance Core*, this guide will help trustees and superintendents adopt a governance mindset and cohesive partnership.